A PRACTICAL GUIDE TO PREACHING

George R. Fitzgerald, C.S.P.

PAULIST PRESS
New York/Ramsey

Acknowledgements
I gratefully acknowledge CBS News for its permission to re-print a News
Commentary by Rod MacLeish (© 1979 CBS Inc. All Rights Reserved), June 2,
1979, and *United Technologies* (Hartford, Connecticut) for its permission to use
Keep It Simple. I am also grateful to Father Thomas Culhane, Pastor of Most Pure
Heart of Mary Church, Topeka, Kansas for permission to re-print a form for
parishioners to use in critiquing the preacher.

Library of Congress
Catalog Card Number: 79-67742

ISBN 0-8091-2281-2

Published by Paulist Press
Editorial Office: 1865 Broadway, N.Y., N.Y. 10023
Business Office: 545 Island Road, Ramsey, N.J. 07446

Published and bound in the
United States of America

Contents

Preface

"A clergyman who could preach was scarcer than a white crow."

Anon. 1471 A.D.

A breakfast conversation where I live at St. Paul the Apostle Rectory in New York City heard an early-side-of forty year old priest render his verdict for the sad state of preaching in the Church: "It's because there are no more good models."

Pursued, as it was with coffee and eggs, this censure has a lot of hidden meaning.

The advent of liturgical reform in the 1960's co-existed with a host of other religious and cultural currents in the society. The sweeping anti-intellectualism in centers of learning in favor of more emotional and rhetorical responses to our political and religious plight did not help traditional values such as preaching. Other factors also had their day. There was a greater sense of equality between laity and clergy and the consequent blurring of roles. And as those who wanted their preaching turn increased in number, we merely added to the host of untrained priests whose own lack of professionalism and training for the pulpit was already a serious pastoral concern. Add to this the diversification of ministries, greater emphasis on personalism and the decline of institutionalism. Liturgies themselves were celebrated more informally, in smaller spaces. Dialogue homilies and shared faith responses grew as custom.

One would have to add to this, of course, the increase in multi-media liturgies when the efforts of priests and staff personnel were directed almost exclusively to hours of planning slide presentations,

1

music, film, etc., with little time left for sermon preparation. Indeed, in some places, media word services pre-empted the sermon. There are other reasons worthy of mention—all of which are quite understandable in a time of religious and societal flip-flop.

To the roster of my friend's verdict against bad preaching, we would have to add general experimentation in word services, in which Scripture often became a stepchild in favor of secular prose and poetry. The general doubt and confusion of the era did not help a discipline such as preaching which presupposes a message to be handed down and proclaimed. What should we proclaim? We're not sure what we believe anymore. Crises of faith, vocation, belief, hope and feelings of religious inadequacy do not form inner incentives to preaching. Parish missions, at least in traditional forms where preaching was central to renewal, collapsed in favor of a catechetical format. This is, of course, what my priest friend meant. When we were kids (and right up through college) it was an event when the missionary came to town. After all, he preached a strong message of conversion; he proclaimed loudly and clearly what grace and God and confession and forgiveness and hell and purgatory were like— and he did so more clearly than our parish priest. Years later I can conjure up for you the images he used. Yes, some of the missionaries were good models. "Gee, I wish I could speak like that," I thought. They knew how to preach; their booming voices reverberated off the vaulted ceilings. They were sure of their faith. No crisis here! "Mother Church's" message came out loud and clear. And then, of course, we had our Fulton Sheen. We saw him every Tuesday night on TV. Say what you want, *there* is a *model!*

Now we're in a different age. Things are a little quieter. People are involved in an intense search for the God within. It's an age of religion. We've gone to Asia for contemplation, listened to the gurus, sought the cults and sects for community and security. Once again we're beginning to get back to some basics, tapping our faith roots, and dusting off the pulpits while we listen to public cries for better preaching.

Seminarians are asking for more preaching courses. Pastoral programs are requiring them of all men asking for ordination. Preaching institutes are cropping up in our land. And a few books *about* preaching (not just collections of sermons) are making their way into bookstores.

My own heightened interest in preaching goes back to the days when Paulist students had to take a course in writing (with emphasis on image words), speech and four years of homiletics. This emphasis in our formation was due, no doubt, to the fact that the Paulists are a missionary community and put strong emphasis on communication (press, radio, and, gradually, TV). The seeds were planted then, and the flower bloomed full when I became rector of our seminary in Washington. There I became interested in pastoral initiatives in seminary formation and responded to an invitation from Sulpician Father Gerry Brown, who headed Catholic University's Pastoral Department, to teach homiletics.

I met Mr. William Graham, who now is at the helm of C.U.'s School of Speech and Drama. Bill and I began to team-teach. I learned more than I taught. Quite singlehandedly, he is responsible for my new interest in proclamation. Many of his ideas are in one form or another in the pages of this book. I shall always be indebted to him.

Nor can I forget Sister Joan Gormley of the Sisters of Notre Dame de Namur. Joan taught Scripture at Trinity and was blessed with the gift of translating Scripture into pastoral language and meanings. I sat as rapt as the students while Joan (with whom I team-taught) told us the various ways a Scripture passage could be preached pastorally.

Added to the fact that theological students do not let rectors get away with very much, my preaching at the seminary got the challenge of its life. Budding theologians form a tough congregation to face. I thank them for that.

These pages, then, are a potpourri of many ideas, people and places, converging into a practical pastoral guide for anyone who wants to improve communication skills in preaching and teaching. Men and women who may never mount the pulpit can find in this book something helpful for catechetics, retreats, communication, speech and reflection. I hope it will be a beginning toward consciousness-raising for good preaching.

I'm grateful to the good friends already cited, as well as to Father Gerry Brown's successors, Fathers Tony Lobo, S.S. and Doug Morrison who renewed the invitation to teach homiletics. For proofreading, typing and various suggestions, my thanks go to Anne-Marie Sullivan, Greg Apparcel and Joe Isola. Finally, I'm grateful to the Paulist Fathers whose preaching tradition has always formed, for me, a catalyst and an ideal, and to Father Kevin Lynch, President of the Paulist Press, who encouraged me to write this book.

It is my hope that those who peruse these pages will come to know and appreciate the full meaning of Boston's famed nineteenth-century Episcopal bishop Phillips Brooks who said that "preaching is bringing truth through personality."

Introduction

PART I: TEN POINTS FOR PREPARATION AND DELIVERY OF SUNDAY SERMONS

1. Make Initial Check.

(a) Next Sunday's texts. Do this on Monday. Read over several times.

(b) Review next week's schedule. Is it heavy? What will Saturday be like? How are you feeling emotionally? Physically? Block out three or four hours for preparation. (As you become more disciplined and confident in your preaching, four hours will not always be necessary. For some occasions, more than four hours will be a must.)

(c) World events, TV shows. Try to get a sense of what media or world events might shape the attitudes of your congregation during the week.

(d) Congregation. What will it be like? Who will be there?

(e) Liturgical Time and Event (Advent, Lent, Pentecost, Ordinary Time). How can this shape my message?

(f) Jottings. Jot down ideas from texts, world events, parish happenings during the week—or anticipated events. Jot down thoughts, feelings, hints, reflections which come to mind during the week.

(g) What ideas come to mind immediately after reading the Scripture selections: stories, examples, associations, comparisons, quotations?

2. Exegete.

(a) Read at least a couple of commentaries. Compare/contrast them. Do new themes or ideas emerge after reading the commentaries? What did the writer intend by the passage? Can a news event fit into this? Does the commentary address any specific pastoral problem? Jot down all possible focuses or themes you could preach on after exegeting the passage.

(b) Delineate your topic and subject. Agree on one main focus, one subject, one topic. Keep the focus narrow, and let it dominate the entire sermon.

(c) Exegete your own life over the past week. What areas of faith, hope, and love emerge as strengths or weaknesses?

3. Personal Experience.

(a) Search through your own personal experiences to which the Scripture message or theme speaks. Jot down reminiscences or memories and stories—your story, someone else's story.

(b) Decide how you want to open your sermon. What will be your attention-gainer? Your "ho-hum crasher"? Ask: "What do I want to be the result of this sermon on my congregation? What's my goal, my aim, my purpose?" If possible, get laypeople in the parish and/or other priests to discuss the passages with you.

4. Meditate, Reflect, Pray.

(a) Take the stories, memories, exegesis, and events of the week and reflect on the ways in which God met you in them. Make some of this the focus of your daily and weekly meditation and reflection.

(b) How do these Scripture passages reflect, similarly, the ways in which God reveals himself to you today—heals, forgives you, is your light, raises you up, etc.?

5. Structure the Sermon.

(a) Outline and block out. Decide on the introduction. Relate this to the curiosity of the listeners, catching and holding interest.

(b) Decide on key words to be repeated throughout the sermon to keep the congregation focused on the theme (observe TV ads: they repeat the product name or catchy phrases for you to remember).

(c) Develop central theme with clear examples: Point one, e.g., point two, e.g., point three, e.g.

(d) Amplify theme with these examples.

(e) Use direct, clear, simple language. Keep it concrete. Use image words.

(f) Cut out theological or philosophical jargon. Be sensitive to avoid sexist language.

(g) For the conclusion, return to the introduction. Summarize and exhort. Connect conclusion to introduction.

6. Write/Rewrite.

(a) Develop the points in the section above. Move from outline to prose development. Keep asking: Could I say this more simply? With more imagery? Review, rewrite, cut. "The wastebasket is the writer's best friend." Cut—even if it means parting with a gem. Ask: Does this sentence or word hinder or help my sermon? Remember: attention not won in the first couple of minutes is never won at all.

(b) Get rid of the "if's," "let us," "shoulds" and "oughts."

7. Stick to Your Scripture Passage.

(a) Use the Scriptures as they are given to you (as an ordinary rule). Probe them. Do not hop, skip and jump all over the Bible to find texts similar to the one you have. Occasionally you might refer to the previous or following passages to context your thought, or allude to the way another evangelist tells the same story. This should be done only in passing rather than in development.

(b) Avoid excessive Scripture quoting except simply, insofar it supports and backs up your theme.

8. Read Aloud.

(a) Practice in front of a mirror. If possible tape or video-tape. Practice over the public address system. Be conscious of your voice.
(b) Underline words you want to emphasize. Keep refining the sermon as you listen to yourself. Get a feel of delivery and a sense of gestures—when they should occur.
(c) Keep asking: Will the congregation know what I mean when I use this or that word? Does it deal with real life? Or is it esoteric? Unrelated? Is it about their life or *speculation* about life? Remember: theology often speculates. The Bible deals with concrete circumstances of human life and the ways in which God breaks in.

9. Conclusion.

(a) Know it well. Concentrate on it. A bad conclusion can ruin a good sermon. Beautiful structures of words and ideas collapse around bad conclusions.
(b) Relate the conclusion to the beginning. Bring the congregation back to your opening. Summarize and exhort, offering practical applications.

10. Critique.

Arrange for a variety of people—young, elderly, married, single, middle-aged, from various education levels—to give you feedback on your sermons. Does your preaching reach them? Do you get the point across? What concrete suggestions can they make to improve your preaching as a pastoral event? Consider video-taping some of the liturgies at which you are the preacher. This will let you see and hear yourself as the congregations experience you.

PART II: EXERCISES AND REFLECTIONS TO ENHANCE PREACHING

1. Do breathing exercises. Learn how to take deep breaths from the diaphragm both for relaxation and for development of good habits in projecting the voice.
2. Before preaching, do some basic relaxation exercises. Standard exercise books are available.
3. Read aloud a Scripture passage a few times a week. Enunciate each word clearly and with emphasis to develop a habit of clear projection, tone and pace. Remember: good speech can be developed through practice.
4. Take a Scripture passage or prose/poetry and go into an auditorium, large church, gymnasium or open field. Shout the passage to the far corners of the area. This exercise is to develop the habit of audible speech, learning to project loudly enough so that the person in the last pew can hear. It emphasizes "proclamation" over "speaking." But remember: Proclamation is not shouting. Proclamation is a special skill.
5. Try full-length mirror practice. Get access to a full-length mirror (every seminary should have a sound-proof room with a full-length mirror), stand in front of it, talk, practice the homily, make faces, gesture freely and extravagantly. This exercise is fun and is given to help the speaker get accustomed to feeling comfortable with his body. Overexaggerate bodily movements, gestures, etc., in order to arrive at a happy medium with which you are comfortable and which is not contrived or artificial.
6. Monitor TV. Pick out two or three television personalities and keep a log on how they speak, words they use, images they form, etc., and observe how they relate to other people on the show. Media people are pros. We can learn from them. TV commercials hit us with action, imagery, repetition, value, all in one minute.
7. Use body language. Be aware, during the week, of the ways in which you walk, sit, and talk. These can be clues to the kind of communicating person you are: involved? distant? impersonal? lethargic? enthusiastic? dynamic? passive? uninterested? What

about your tone of voice, pitch, resonance, rate, rhythm, personal appearance, clothing? What signals are you picking up from people with whom you relate during the week? Involvement? Avoidance? Are you active and involved or reclusive and withdrawn?

8. Ask someone to critique you once during the week on some of the points noted above. How does this person see you? Experience you?

9. Read Scripture for fifteen minutes every day. Try to visualize persons, places, environment of the passage, the inter-relationship of biblical characters with Jesus and each other. Retell out loud, to yourself, what is happening in the passage. Note, especially in the breviary, the strong image and concrete language of the psalms, of the prophets, of Jesus. Study the words used. Write down image words and build up a file on them. Make this Scripture reading *active* reading.

10. When you feel that you've mastered some of the above, start thinking of training people in the parish to be lectors. Build up a core group of public "proclaimers" in the parish. This will enhance their own lives, as well as the faith life of the community.

1.
Subject and Theme

"Yet preaching the Gospel is not the subject of a boast; I am under compulsion and have no choice. I am ruined if I do not preach it."

1 Cor. 9:16

"If a hundred thousand Christs had been crucified and no one said anything about it, what use would that have been?"

Martin Luther

"It must be narrow enough to be sharp."

H. Grady Davis

It is Sunday. I have just finished preaching at all of the Masses. I'm tired. The week ahead stares me in the face. Next Sunday I'm preaching again. As a matter of fact, I'm preaching at three daily Masses this week. I'm tied up all day Tuesday, Wednesday and Thursday in meetings, evening classes and appointments. There's a funeral on Tuesday. Tomorrow, Monday, maybe I'd better look at next Sunday's readings and start thinking about them—jot some ideas down and look at the *Jerome Biblical Commentary*. What a week ahead! Wonder what I'll preach about?

Each week—for some preachers, each day—a decision has to be made: What single thought do I wish to leave with the congregation? Out of all the ideas in these two or three Scripture passages for next Sunday, out of the events of the week, out of the congregation's experiences and my own, what single emphasis will speak most strongly to the people in the pews?

Critical Faith Moment

This decision is crucial. For most of the congregation, the preaching event is the single most important catechetical time of the week. You have from five to fifteen golden minutes to touch their lives in a significant way. Your words can open their hearts to conversion by the Spirit, help them respond to God's action in their lives and to experience the nearness of the Lord. During these few precious pastoral moments, you have the chance to move hundreds of people toward thanksgiving, love, hope, and freedom from fear, and to experience forgiveness. For some, it will be the most important and memorable faith experience of the week. Lives may be changed. Some deeper meaning may be given to life.

That's a big order for a big opportunity. It requires a lot from me as preacher. Like Paul speaking to the Thessalonians, we are commissioned to call our congregations "through our preaching of the good news so that you might achieve the glory of our Lord Jesus Christ." It is tougher, still, because many Catholics have written off good preaching as an expectation of their worshiping experience. For them, the faith moment of the week is centered around the moment of consecration. That's what they expect and know will happen, regardless of who preaches.

Practical Beginning: Personal Faith Experience

The beginning of my task is practical. I first make a commitment to the subject and theme. I search my own faith, reflecting on the Scriptures of the week. I ask myself: "How can I say what I must, speaking with enthusiasm about what I believe? How is this particular passage re-enacted in my own life?" While I do not advocate preaching about myself (a homily filled with "I's"), the faith I preach must come out of my own experience of God in my life. It is he whom I preach, in the persons of Father, Son and Spirit, and it must be he who comes through in my own faith experience. I meet God in the day-to-day happenings of my life—through people, events, conflicts, silence, prayer, doubt. The focus of my preaching is on what God has done to and for me. When I finish preaching, the congregation should be focused on God, not on me; and reflected through me should be God's action in *their own* lives.

As you choose a theme and subject, know what it is that excites you about the faith expression that greets you in Scripture. Ask yourself: "Can I retell the story with excitement and enthusiasm?" Remember, we are most moved when someone preaches to us about what has happened in a most personal and exciting way in his or her own life. John Henry Newman said it well: "Heart speaks to heart."

In the evangelical programs on TV, I am always touched by hearing people of all ages, colors and backgrounds relate, in simple, personal, unaffected language, the ways in which they meet Jesus in their own lives. The power of their words rests in the sincerity and depth of what they believe. I, as listener, may not agree or be able to identify with their faith experience; I may not be able even to share my own faith as personally as they do. But to hear them often challenges me to look at my own faith. I sense that these people *really* believe what they are saying. There is strength in that. They are not reading what someone else has written about God. What they say comes from their hearts. So, too, the preacher's words must come from the heart to reach other hearts.

Recurrent Themes in the Old and New Testaments

Knowing the congregation will help to determine the subject and theme of our preaching. Becoming familiar with the recurrent themes which orchestrate most of Scripture can be helpful, too. These themes point to human situations which God addresses over and over again.

As an exercise, take a look at a *Concordance* to learn how often certain key words in Scripture reflect our human experience, as well as the universal human experience. Several pages are devoted singly to such themes as: *forgiveness, being found, fear, feast, feed, bread, love, judgment, hope, thanksgiving, joy, righteousness, save, savior, prayer, praise, preach, faith, take, spirit, speak, son, daughter, death, heal, hear, heart, holy, life, longing, looking, Lord, man, woman, word, work, world, wrath, wilderness, whole, weep/weeping, walk/*

walking, water, neighbor, met, give, gate, gather, harvest, grain, food, God, follow, flesh, fire, find, fall, face/faced, eyes, seek, save/saved, satisfy, poor, possess/possessed, pleased and *peace.*

So many of these are related to the common joys, anxieties and hopes of the human family to which God addresses himself again and again. They are words which occur frequently in the sacramental rites of the Church, as well as the various canons of the eucharistic liturgy. The preacher's message is enhanced when he touches the common experiences of people everywhere. Everyday experiences, such as eating, searching, healing, loving and dying are blind to position and status in life. They cut across and through every human heart. Preaching must touch on the dimensions of our lives that are most personal, and often the most unsettled. For many people, preaching stirs positive feelings of gratitude related to fruitful personal searching, remembrance of meaning in moments of crisis and memories of moments when things came together in their personal lives.

God Is Near

One of the aims of preaching is to help people become aware that God is near, even in the strange mixture of good and evil all around them. He is near to every expression of their heart and mind. People come to Mass to be fed—both with the word of God in Scripture and through the Eucharist. St. Paul tells us that "the word is near to you, on your lips and in your heart." The aim of preaching is to help people discover the nearness of God who is already within, written on the tablets of flesh in their hearts.

People need to hear that message over and over again. For many it is the only truth that makes life bearable. It is the thin edge between despair and hope. "Come to me, all you who are burdened and heavy-hearted, and I will give you rest."

The words that God reveals to us say something about his compassionate care and concern for his people. In addition to individual words cited earlier for their frequency in the *Concordance,* significant themes orchestrate these common words of Scripture: giving/taking/receiving, working/resting, being born/dying/being born again, burdens imposed/burdens lifted, sin/forgiveness, temptation/

temptation resisted, hungry/being filled, thirst/drink, poverty/ abundance, exile/returning home, waiting/fulfillment, expectation/patience, broken/wholeness, sickness/healing, blindness/sight, lame/walk, fear/peace, darkness/light, slavery/liberation, lost/save.

Human Needs: The Shaping of Pastoral Response

Each one of us experiences some of these human moods and needs. They shape our lives and follow us wherever we go. The most pious, most holy, most joyful, most sinful, most forgiven—all share one thing: a hunger and thirst to love and be loved. That is what frees each of us to know God. The most enlightened persons often feel blind and ignorant; they doubt themselves, what they believe and even what they hold most dear.

We are tempted a hundred times daily—tempted toward greed, egotism, self-righteousness, exploitative relationships, destructive sexuality, doubt and despair. Even in our triumphs we feel guilty, broken and in need of healing, in need of purity of heart and humility. We need the Spirit to lift us up from our failures, to bring the fragments together.

The physically and emotionally ill desperately feel the need for bodily healing and religious healing of the Spirit as well—to fathom God's purposes and the mysteries of life and death.

In the course of our lives we wait for a thousand things. We wait for persons (some of whom never come), for the moment of success, for that "one and only" to come into our lives, for that bonus, that assignment, that promotion. We wait for the once-in-a-lifetime vacation. We see poverty all around us and paradoxically awaken to abundance. What does this say about our social responsibility as Christians? We want to help others but don't know how. The economic and political structures of the world appear too huge and awesome to tackle. What can we do in the face of such power?

Sunday after Sunday, the pews and pulpits are filled with men, women and children who struggle for peace in their hearts, in their homes and in the world. Together we feel enslaved by fears, by our wants, our needs, our hates and our pettiness. We seek liberation. Whether we know it or not, we seek a Savior. In faith, we know that we are saved by the blood of Jesus—that he has already done it for us. Yet at times we feel lost, wishing to be found again. Jesus seems so far away. God's footprints are being covered with sand and dust. All around us—and in ourselves—we see and find salvation in drugs, alcohol, and possessions, in gurus, strange cults and false promises of salvation. Like Paul, there is much "that tickles our ears." We have "the desire to do right, but not the power." We won't—we cannot truly believe we are saved. We are at home but feel in exile; we want to go home again, somehow.

Day after day, Sunday after Sunday, season after season, these themes of life dominate Scripture and the liturgical cycles of the Church year. Since the purpose of Jesus was to reconcile us to the Father's friendship through forgiveness and a share in his kingdom of grace on earth, it is no wonder that the parables and healing stories are a motif on the theme of forgiveness which, biblically speaking, points to resurrection and hope. The preacher's task is to mine the meaning often hidden in those simple biblical stories.

The Week in Review

When I sit down to prepare a sermon and search for a theme, it is likely that some personal experience of an individual or event will be reflected in the readings. As I probe my experience of the past week or of recent memory, I seek some alliance between that experience and what I discover in the pages of Scripture. I ask: "Do the people, events, dilemmas, situations in the biblical readings for today, or next Sunday, reflect something of my own life?" In all likelihood, the answer is "yes."

What about the congregation? What might they have experienced during the past week which unites them in their questions, hopes or fears? Maybe they have experienced what you have experienced—perhaps in slightly different ways. Come out of your faith—and theirs—and people will listen. Let them know you understand their hopes and fears, their doubts and faith, their struggles to bring God closer to their lives. Let your experience speak to theirs—and God will speak to both. When you finish, the congregation will be more aware of what God has done in and for you, and can do for them. Sermons on human events, Vatican Council documents, political/moral issues—all of these can be contexted within Scripture and religious experiences of the people. They can be springboards for hope and for understanding how God works in and through history.

Choice of Topic: Effects of World Events

As the preacher faces preparation of a sermon, several choices present themselves. For example, the occurrences of the week may demand some comment. Often news of such impact on everyone's lives cannot be sidestepped. Human events raise questions which address themselves directly to religion. Events such as the assassination of President John Kennedy, the gripping cold and personal suffering and hardship of the winter of 1977, the assassinations of Martin Luther King and Robert Kennedy, the Begin-Sadat meeting in Jerusalem just prior to Thanksgiving 1977, and the peace talks at Camp David just nine months later—all of these struck at the core of what is essentially religious in all of us. A more recent event, bewildering to people's religious sensitivities, was the mass suicides of the People's Temple cult of Rev. Jim Jones in Guyana.

Each of these events dominated the news. History perched on tragedy, expectation, disappointment, hope and fear. These news items were the talk of the town in homes, buses, subways, at schools, in doctor's offices—everywhere. Deep emotions stirred—emotions of confusion, hatred, cynicism and skepticism. Personal faith and belief in God and religion were questioned. Some of these events brought the world together in a partnership of grief, hope and anxiety. We felt both our weaknesses and our vulnerability. We were most in need of faith at these times: an affirmation that God is near, that he is to be sought and found somewhere in this mire of daily quest and human heartbreak.

Local and Parish Events:
Sources of Faith and Hope

The preacher may choose to seize on a local news event that has seriously affected the parish or community: the death of a teenager in an automobile accident, a fire which has taken several lives, or some other traumatic event in the town or city. A joyous occasion could elicit a sermon on thanksgiving, gratitude or the sharing of common hopes. It is the preacher's task to bring new perspectives of hope even out of tragedy and sadness, to reconcile conflicting human emotions within a worshiping community struggling to make sense out of what happens and appears to make no sense.

In one small town, the parish priest decided to center a celebration around the hundredth birthday of a parishioner who was well known and who was still able to attend Mass each week. This vigorous, optimistic lady became the center of the parish's attention for a day of celebration: a Mass of thanksgiving, an open parish party, and even performances by parish and local talent. The priest preached beautifully on the grace of aging and how elderly people become sources of faith for us by their wisdom, experience and patience. No one in the parish had ever heard a sermon on aging until that day. And they never forgot it!

Another less happy occasion came when a woman in the parish lost her five children in a fire. The deaths nearly paralyzed the little community. Not one pew was empty on the day of the funeral. The mother, who was divorced and now completely alone, chose the Gospel story which tells us that "your treasure is where your heart is."

In the midst of this unbelievable tragedy, the mother of the dead children had the faith and peace of mind to stand before the five white caskets and the congregation and say that she finally understood what God was talking about in this parable. Everything may be taken away, but your treasure is to be found where your heart is. All her treasures had been taken away—all that she had—but suddenly she had discovered another treasure, in her heart. It was her faith—a faith that God would see her through this loss and light up her future with hope; that was now her "treasure."

The preacher joined her in reflecting on that passage. She then told that congregation that she and her children had been practicing some sacred dance together at home. It was one way the six of them prayed together. She now wanted to do that dance, she said, as a final tribute to her children. She danced, quietly and in good taste, around the caskets and into the sanctuary, her hands and body movements a silent prayer of trust in God. Her own faith, needless to say, strengthened all who were there. It was an unforgettable faith moment in the midst of shattering tragedy.

Obviously, this is a rare happening. Most people couldn't do that. It demonstrated, however, the power of a person's faith and had a deep impact on everyone—believer and unbeliever alike.

Another example of using a local event occurred in a small rural community which had been devastated by floods. The churches, historically divided into their petty acrimonies, had not yet ever worked together for any purpose. Suddenly, faced with disaster, the priests and ministers stirred the townspeople by their preaching. They mobilized people to set up rescue centers on church properties, went around comforting people, held joint prayer services and exchanged pulpits. Such an occasion warranted a sermon on the power of reconciliation, how good rose from tragedy, how God traced his lines through plans of action in the community, in the midst of tragedy and loss. Ecumenism and community action based on the faith response of the people was no longer an abstraction. It was real, visible, tangible. People felt good about it. It was an example of faith in action, and no one compromised any religious beliefs. The event converted religion in that little town from a routine Sunday morning event to a shared community experience that made the Beatitudes come alive.

The death of a child in a community, especially if sudden and tragic, or apparently meaningless, also calls for some homiletic event. People are asking, "Why does God let this happen?" I am surprised at how many priests in the Catholic Church sidestep any comment at a funeral where hundreds of people, with a potpourri of religious beliefs, are present and need to hear someone of faith give real meaning to the event. Their faith (or lack of it) is being tested. Life appears meaningless. The bottom has dropped out of their world. The sensitive pastor can be of great help at this time. His preaching can reassure the people that God is still near to them. It is a prized moment to preach on suffering and the cross as a part of the mystery of God saving us. Texts on Jesus and the little children are powerful here as well. The pulpit can be charged with grace and hope at times such as this if the preacher is open to the action of such grace.

Problem Solving from the Pulpit

Problem-solving sermons can be helpful, too. The preacher may focus on the real concerns of the faithful. Harry Emerson Fosdick calls this "life-situation" preaching. He believes that every sermon should have, as its main business, the solving of a problem—an important problem that puzzles minds, distracts people's lives or burdens their consciences. These are problems associated with human tragedy, death, family, civic affairs, dissension in the community, factions, etc. Any attempt to unravel a problem which people are feeling, Fosdick believes, cannot be that uninteresting, for people are always seeking answers, and to help them solve their spiritual problems is a sermon's only justifiable aim.

Some preachers disagree with such a categorical statement, but it is, I think, at least a justifiable aim. For Fosdick, the preacher does not necessarily start with some biblical text. He starts with a human need which he sees and then proceeds to solve the problem arising out of that need. For example, if people need to be consoled in a grief situation, the preacher finds the Scripture passage that speaks to this human feeling. Some of Fosdick's reasons are pragmatic, growing out of a belief that the modern congregation could not care less about the Philistines or the Jebusites or about demons being driven out.

For Catholic, Lutheran and Episcopalian preachers it is important to stay with the seasonal texts. Their liturgies follow a calendar, and preachers should be very reluctant to interrupt that cycle, unless a dramatic occasion offers an option for special readings to meet the human need. Baptisms, weddings, funerals, and liturgies for civic occasions and for various needs fall into that latter category. Some problem-solving preaching might be construed as a revolt against fundamentalism in religion—from a God-centered to a man-centered preaching.

The two need not be exclusive. There is no reason why a solid, biblically-based sermon addressing a modern problem cannot be presented. The Gospel need not be left out. The Bible addresses *every* human problem. Maybe that's a clue to its being the world's best seller.

Liturgical Themes

The preacher can also be effective when he appeals to the faith of the people as it is lived and deepened within the liturgical rhythms of the community's worship life. During Advent and Lent especially, there is a heightened sense of participation in the congregation. Clear themes are discernible in the Scriptures. The great feasts of the Church touch deep and personal human feelings. Preaching on these same feelings, experienced by our religious forebears, creates a sense of shared faith: a sense that we are all part of a larger religious heritage in the long pilgrimage of man's searching for and awaiting a Savior.

Advent heightens our sense of waiting, expectation and promise—and waiting is a large part of life. Daily, we await the birth of Jesus in our hearts and to see him in new ways in our lives. Advent, as a liturgical season, is a moment in the Church's worship calendar which attunes us more sensitively to that part of our lives which is always advent—which is always waiting, expecting and hoping.

Christmas celebrates all of those moments in our lives when waiting has been fulfilled in event. Christmas is the promise fulfilled; God does not leave us alone. We see God in Jesus, "with our own eyes," the Christmas Preface says. Christmas is a good day to preach on the many ways in which God breaks through into our world as he becomes one of us and reveals himself in Jesus.

Epiphany lends itself to the same theme—the many showings of Jesus, and the recognition of him as Messiah by wise men from another religious culture. We jump from the Christmas theme of Jesus being born into our lives to the ways in which we, in our lives, manifest Jesus to others. We move from Advent (expectation) to Christmas (birth) to Epiphany (manifestation).

Lent is a good time to preach on the place of sacrificial love and repentance in a lived, dynamic religion. Its themes place conversion at the center of faith so that we may experience the many ways in which the risen Lord calls us daily from dyings and deaths to hopes for new directions, new ways of seeing things and new faith energies. Pentecost invites sermons which focus on the ways in which we experience renewal and re-creation in our lives. Trinity Sunday is a superb moment to speak of our faith as a community experience, lived not alone but in relationship to others, with the hope and promise that come from interaction with others, just as God is communitarian in a Trinity of three persons relating through love and creativity.

Preaching on the lives of the saints in daily liturgies can provide models for the people. The lives of the saints, many of whom lived in times of turmoil, and who responded to every detailed human situation we face, can provide hope to the listener. The lives of the saints personalize faith and make it real by removing faith for us from the abstractions of theology.

The great feast days and liturgical cycles present themes that grow out of our common needs. Year after year these feast days celebrate and highlight the same recurrent rhythms in our lives, just as nature's seasons direct our eyes and ears to the beauty and order of creation. We who are believing people need to keep hearing about expectation, birth, sacrificial love and repentance, because none of these are ever completely fulfilled in our lives. We need to experience and reflect, again and again, on these human needs as the stuff of our faith. They are perennial feelings, always present. That's why the Church's liturgical cycle keeps repeating itself, like nature's seasons, to keep that life alive. We are part of that ever-recurrent rhythm.

Stay with the Scripture Text

Whatever the specific topical focus of the preacher, there is no substitute for staying with the given text. Every story in Scripture is a human experience of God. The experience may be told through a dream, an imaginative scene, a parable, a healing story, or a moment of forgiveness. Each experience focuses on a human need deep within each of us. The preacher who says to his congregation "This passage leaves me cold," or "I can't get anything out of this passage so I'm going to forego preaching today" commits a cardinal sin of ministry. The lectionary selections, evolved after centuries of use and revision, have grown out of a common faith experience. Many were used as catechesis in the formative years of the Church. They represent the Church's creed and its hopes. The Church, which hears those Scriptures, nurtures, and is nurtured by, them. It stands under their judgment.

When a preacher abdicates preaching on difficult or apparently meaningless passages, he, in effect, admits to the people that what God has said in that passage is helpless to reach his listeners. He pushes the word under a bushel basket. Simple exegesis or a biblical commentary would have offered some hint at what the passage meant, why the writer chose the words he did, to whom and what culture he was speaking, and to what human dilemma these words were spoken. A simple discussion with someone else about the Scripture passage could have opened up avenues of wisdom for this discouraged pulpit mentor. To announce that Scripture means nothing is to allow light to be smothered by darkness and hope swallowed up in despair. If, after work and exegesis, prayer and counsel, a particular passage still means absolutely nothing, the preacher can, without comment, simply sit down for quiet reflection. The people will follow suit.

Selection of Texts

Good pastoral practice admits that occasions will demand some change in the Scripture passages given to us in the Ordo. This should be done only for good pastoral reason. There was a period during heightened (and often casual) liturgical experimentation in the early years following Vatican II to introduce, as common practice, the shelving of daily and Sunday liturgies in favor of selected readings culled from Scripture and other literary sources. Themes were chosen to fit the mood or feeling of the week. It is true that certain moments in the life of congregations can be enhanced by this practice. The problem is that preachers and congregations are too easily relieved of hearing or struggling with Scripture. This practice makes the challenge of hearing God's word too easy, too packaged and too selective. Such a habit of selection would never allow us to identify with Jacob, who had to wrestle with an angel before receiving God's blessing. To sidestep the passages given us in the liturgy can easily degenerate into cheap and easy grace—perhaps too soothing, too agreeable, too uncostly, dulling the two-edged sword which Scripture must be.

In the celebration of the sacraments, the liturgy encourages selection from a variety of texts given in the lectionary. It may be that on occasions such as baptism the preacher wants to select passages more pastorally suited to the occasion. Readings about Jesus' relationship to children would be more suited to the baptism of children than adults. Likewise, in marriage, a celebrant or preacher may feel that the passage on divorce (the only option, by the way, in the unreformed liturgy) is inappropriate on a wedding day when the couple's love is focused on fidelity and permanence, rather than separation and disunity.

To Speak with Authority

Apart from being a sheer cop-out to announce that the Scriptures have "nothing to say to me" or "I don't understand them," it is atrocious communication. A preacher who announces this to the congregation invites a similar response from them: "Well, Father, if you have nothing to say, or the Scripture passage doesn't mean anything to you, I'm not going to waste my time listening to whatever it is you have to say."

One could hardly imagine Jesus getting up before the crowds on the hillsides to announce, "Well, folks, I have nothing to say," or, "I'm not prepared today; you'll have to get your own loaves and fishes."

People who comprise our congregations want to be fed the word as they are fed the Eucharist. "I ate the scroll" with the word of God written on it, says Ezekiel, "and it tasted sweet as honey."

The crowds in the pews wait for the preacher to "speak with authority." That does not mean to speak with authoritarian airs or to have all the answers. It does mean that they expect him to share the authority of one educated and trained and ordained to preach God's Word, and for him to have pondered the word so that he can speak with conviction. The congregation has every right to expect the preacher to have "pondered" the Word before entering the pulpit, to preach with fervor, to "deliver my words to them whether they listen or not," as God commanded Ezekiel. The mandate is the same for every ordained minister.

Related to this is the practice of side-stepping the sermon because an appeal or a letter from the bishop is seen to take precedence on a particular Sunday. It is my belief that *nothing* justifies shelving the sermon. An appeal can be made or a letter read at various times in the Mass. When pastoral necessity requires an appeal or a letter, a homily should precede it. Perhaps the appeal and letter can be integrated into the sermon itself. When the two are separate, a three- to five-minute homily should be given. People come to Mass to be fed. They are asking for bread, for strength, in the week to come, and they deserve to get what they ask for. The Church sees the Sunday readings as catechesis, instructions for deepening and improving the faith and life of its believers. The preaching moment is so vital as to take a prominent and never secondary place in the liturgy of the word.

Identity with Persons in Scripture

Finally, the question: With whom should the preacher identify in Scripture—Jesus or the person to whom Jesus ministers?

There's a long tradition that the preacher should identify with Jesus, as well as a developing mood that he should identify with the person receiving Jesus' concern. I say that we should do both.

Identify with the kind of person Jesus was: imitate his forgiveness, compassion, gentleness, humility, and mercy. Be faithful to God the Father as he was. Imitate his availability, his need to go off into the desert for quiet prayer and reflection. Jesus is the ministering person par excellence. The preacher's own care will grow from seeing Jesus as model.

On the other hand, identifying with the people to whom Jesus ministers helps us to see ourselves as those persons who need and ask for Jesus to come into our own lives. We are the lame man, the daughter of the widow of Naim, the man born blind, Lazarus, the beggar, Martha, Mary, the man possessed by demons. We are the repentant thief, the woman at the well, the crowds waiting to be fed. We are impetuous Peter, doubting Thomas, curious Zacchaeus. These people are microcosms of us. Their lives reflect our own.

The attitude of identifying with the people to whom Jesus ministered rather than with Jesus does not always square with a long respected tradition within the ascetical theology of vocation, namely, that the priest is another Christ—an "alter Christus." This theology, however, grew out of a theology of vocation and ordination which identified the priest with Jesus in a very special way. While there are many elements of this theology of priesthood which have strong appeal in helping priests to model their lives after Jesus, it can lead to arrogance in ministry and in the misuse of authority. Who, after all, can challenge the claims of "another Christ"? Certainly not anyone in the congregation.

St. Paul believed himself to be the "least of the apostles." John the Baptist said he was "unworthy to loosen the sandal straps" of Jesus. Somewhere along the line, Catholic piety elevated the priest to an almost superhuman level of relationship with Jesus. This makes it difficult for the priest to identify, publicly, with the same human problems which beset the people in the pews. Thus the priest, as preacher, mounted the pulpit speaking as if Jesus were speaking. He claimed almost the same authority. I believe that identity with those same persons who receive the saving words and acts of Jesus is a stronger faith platform for the preacher. This identity with biblical characters compels us to struggle with the word of God in our own lives. It lends itself to reflectiveness about experiences which can effectively be translated into words of hope and encouragement to the congregation. We then become the *receiver* of God's grace in the pulpit, shared through our preaching and reflection, more than the *dispenser* of it, as "other Christs."

Conclusion

So much for subject and theme. Obviously the choice is wide and varied. The narrower the focus, the better. The more rooted in Church tradition, the better. The time we spend, the effort at discipline and reflection, the setting aside of a special time for preparation, the continual orchestration of the theme and subject throughout the sermon—all these will spell the difference between a congregation that is inert and dead or alert and alive. As a first decision in the preaching moment—that of preparation, subject and theme—it will signal to your congregation whether you take them, and the sacred word of Scripture, seriously. Nothing could be better in earning their eyes and ears, and sending them home rich in hope.

SPECIFIC POINTS AND EXERCISES FOR STUDY

From POINTS FOR PREPARATION AND DELIVERY (See *Introduction* I)

   I. Make initial check:
   (a) Next Sunday's texts. Do this on Monday. Read over several times.
   (b) World events, TV shows. Try to get a sense of what media or world events might shape the attitudes of your congregation during the week.
   (c) Liturgical Time and Event (Advent, Lent, Pentecost, Ordinary Time). How can this shape my message?

  II. Jot down all possible themes. Delineate your topic and subject. Decide what point you want to make. Narrow your focus. Ask: What one or two clear points do I want to leave with my congregation?

 III. Pick out a point or two from the Scripture reading for next Sunday's sermon and make it the focus of your daily meditation and reflection. Mull over this idea while walking, sitting quietly, praying, taking a shower, lying in bed for a few moments before dropping off to sleep.

  IV. What ideas come to mind immediately after reading the Scripture selections: stories, examples, associations, comparisons, quotations?

   V. Ask how you can identify with the person or persons to whom Jesus or God (Old Testament) is relating. What is their state of mind? Their condition of faith? How am I like them?

  VI. Think of a faith experience in which God was strongly present to you. Tell yourself (aloud) or someone else the story. As an interesting facet to the telling, try to keep God in the center of the story rather than yourself.

From EXERCISES AND REFLECTIONS TO ENHANCE PREACHING (See *Introduction* II)

I. Do breathing exercises. Learn how to take deep breaths from the diaphragm, both for relaxation and for development of good habits in projecting the voice.

II. Before preaching, do some basic relaxation exercises. Standard exercise books are available.

2.
Critique of Self as a Communicating Person

"What happens is that I do, not the good I will to do, but the evil I do not intend."

Rom. 7:19.

"That God's saving word should be believed does not depend on us but we can do very much toward making it respected."

Etienne Gilson

William Manchester's book *American Caesar* vividly paints the twilight years of Douglas MacArthur. In a touching scene, captured both in the book and a movie, MacArthur sounds his final "roll call" to the West Point cadets: "I want you to know that when I cross the river, my last conscious thought will be of the Corps, and the Corps, and the Corps. I bid you farewell."

The awed cadets thought that the General was coining each phrase off the top of his head. But what they had actually witnessed, says Manchester, "was the last performance of a consummate actor who always wrote his own lines beforehand, honed and polished them and committed them to memory."

A friend of MacArthur recalled seeing him "pacing like a brooding hawk . . . puffing a corncob as he rehearsed," memorizing every word of that "performance."

What a lesson for preachers!

MacArthur was a great orator. Americans remember him for his ability to stir the passions of war-torn peoples through quiet, impassioned rhetoric. As a college freshman, I remember his address before Congress in 1951 after President Truman recalled him from the Far East. "Old soldiers never die," he said. "They just fade away." The words moved Americans as few have ever done.

A listener might sit back in envy and say, "Gee, I wish I could speak like that." Well, maybe you can. But first you have to write.

MacArthur did what every good preacher begins by doing. He committed his words to paper. The preacher who does not write is in danger of becoming slipshod in style, limited in vocabulary, superficial in thought and helter-skelter in aim. Writing out the sermon (even though you may not intend to memorize or read it) enhances the possibility of sharper image. Writing commits you to words and ideas which have been thought through, prayed and reflected over. As the preacher writes, he keeps in mind the core idea which is to dominate and give the sermon its unity—like MacArthur! He searches for and writes down key words he will want the congregation to remember. Writing allows him to aim more directly, to be precise in meaning, to polish his ideas with verbal form. Writing allows the preacher to keep a coherent development of words and images throughout the sermon. Writing is an anchor, a compass, a sail that allows the preacher to control, direct, and pursue a course of development. Most bad sermons are bad because they aim at nothing and hit at nothing . . . or everything. The preacher who does not write can rarely ever hope to achieve quality and greatness in proclamation. The person speaking to you so personally on TV is usually reading something written on a monitor or "idiot" cards. It has been prepared. The genius of the speaker is to communicate with you in such a personal way that you do not allude to the fact of a written message. The preacher has to do the same. He should know his written material so well that the congregation is not conscious that it is in front of him.

MacArthur made it sound all so easy. There was nothing contrived, loud, theatrical, hyper-emotional or sentimentally vapid about his words. They stirred the heart through an appeal to a universal human emotion, centered on the will to win and to survive through appeal to the qualities of patriotism, honor and loyalty. MacArthur knew his people and he knew where to touch them.

Hours and hours of reflection brought him to that point of knowledge; equal amounts of practice enabled him to master the podium, as few American heroes have ever done. What MacArthur had was self-discipline, an ability to write and the will to practice, to practice, and to practice. "The Corps, and the Corps, and the Corps. . . . "

Preaching As Art

Good—or great—speaking is an art. Like any art, there are rules, norms, guidelines and procedures which define its perfection. An artist paints and paints again; he begins a work which he might never finish. He starts over. He observes others and is often dissatisfied with his own work. He reflects on the genius of those who have made their name in artistic circles. "Why have they achieved perfection in their art and not I?" he asks. The better he masters the skills of his trade, however, the more likely people will judge him well, as they did MacArthur. He made it sound so easy, as if it all had come from improvisation. But it had not. It had come from practice—and from writing.

The same applies to the preacher. By virtue of his vocation, he is a communicator of the word. He has no real choice in the matter. He may decide, however, that he does not like preaching. He does not want to expend the discipline required for good preaching—reading, practicing, prayer, acquiring good speech patterns. But when he so decides, it will be a decision that runs counter to the commission given him by the people, through the bishop, at ordination:

"Receive the Gospel of Christ, whose herald you are."

"Now you must not only listen to God's word but also preach it. Express in action what you proclaim by word of mouth."

It is clear that the ordained minister has been chosen—chosen to preach. There's very little room to wriggle out of that clear commitment. And if he can't preach, he can *learn* to preach.

Learning to Preach

"To *learn* how to preach? I doubt it's possible. Either you're a good preacher or you're not; either you can or you can't." So say many who seem to know.

It is true that certain personality types are gifted with the charism of communicating with the spoken word. Some individuals enjoy talking with others. They like people. They are "at home" in the pulpit and public speaking fits them like a glove. Words are pleasant company, and images flow gracefully from them, moving their audience into new worlds through imagination, persuasion and uplifting grace.

However, the fact is that most people, gifted or not, start somewhere at the end of the spectrum of shyness, amid a lack of self-confidence, reticence and nervousness, as they begin their education and training for public ministry. Unless a person is unique, those familiar gastro-intestinal stirrings are uncomfortable reminders of his fallibility in pastoral ministry and the pulpit. Most people are not born with the gift of rhetoric or persuasion. Sermons come from hard work, a lot of ego investment, a dose of sweat, a strong commitment to practice, and a belief that the Holy Spirit supports and urges us on.

Belief in Oneself

In an introductory preaching class I taught a few years ago, a shy, retiring young man began to deliver his first homily. All the hearts of his listeners went out to him but he couldn't continue. I assured him that this was all right. I asked, however, that he try to give the same homily the following week. I gave him some practice exercises to do during the week, but he was convinced he would never be able to preach. Fear and depression were the result of his first attempt.

This young man worked hard. He wrote and taped his sermons, delivered them to friends, and practiced in front of a mirror. He subsequently became a first-rate preacher. His sincerity and warmth came through his words. He drew on personal experience as a vehicle for his faith. Although some nervousness remained, it never became obtrusive. The student congregation became aware of, and responded to, his faith, rather than his nervousness. He developed and learned a pastoral skill.

This young man's growth as a preacher was born, first, of a conviction that preaching is important. He invested time during the week. He sought help. It was hard work and belief in himself that rescued him from that first day's disaster.

Other students often begin in the same way. When they believe in themselves and the importance of preaching and when they are convinced that they owe their congregations every ounce of effort during these years of preparation, they will become good preachers.

Various Preaching Aids

There are a number of avenues to take. Articles and books on basic communication skills are a helpful beginning. Speech courses and speaking exercises are often invaluable in building confidence. Other exercises include practicing in front of a mirror, getting critiqued, doing breathing exercises, becoming aware of yourself as a communicating person in other circumstances besides preaching, reading Scripture aloud, tape-recording your voice, watching yourself on a video screen, and working to express yourself clearly and concisely in any verbal encounter. Good preaching is ninety-nine percent hard work; the rest is God's grace.

Good Speech: Consciousness Raising

When I was studying philosophy in 1960, each Paulist seminarian was required to take speech courses from Mrs. Josephine Callan at Catholic University. Mrs. Callan had coached hundreds of students in drama. She taught them how to project their voices so that listeners in the far corners of the theatre could hear them. She taught her students to speak with clarity, as well as how to use words and gestures to reach and move people, both intellectually and emotionally. She coached us on how to proclaim the Scriptures, and even gave simple exercises for us to do while walking, sitting, showering— all as part of the plan for us to become conscious of ourselves as communicators. Her motto was: "Practice, practice, practice. Be conscious of yourself speaking clearly." She helped us to believe that each one could become a good speaker with work and discipline. Voice projection, clear speech, intonation, variation, and word emphasis are skills to be learned, she said. She helped us to develop our imagination so that we could approach Scripture in the richness of the world in which the event took place. Reading poetry aloud was a beginning exercise for the imagination. She directed her remarks to us as future preachers, working to make us believe that good preaching requires respect for professional communication skills, just as a religious artist or sculptor needs to shape his own understanding of his religious characters so that the viewer will receive his world of faith and be moved by it.

Mrs. Callan caught our individual styles. She helped us to strengthen those styles, convincing us that the imitation of others (such as Fulton Sheen) was not the way to good preaching. The telling of a truth, I found, should differ in some way for each person telling it. And to develop one's own style, according to one's own faith and personality, is essential to authentic preaching. Too many people preach in a way that is consistent with something they have read or heard, but without it first filtering through themselves, and without first taking the time to translate it into terms of their own uniqueness.

A Paulist priest joined Mrs. Callan in this effort. During his several years as instructor in writing and speech, he emphasized image words and short clear sentences. He projected our themes on a screen and shared his critique with all of us. To raise our consciousness of speech, he would take us to the football field, he at one end and we at the other, while he listened to us project our voices across the expanse of the field. There were no bullhorns or electrical amplifiers used. Gradually we developed a sense of the need to be heard, to speak clearly, to aim our remarks at the person in the last pew, so that everyone could hear. If that most distant person can hear, then it is likely that everyone else will, too.

I believe, too, that an examination of one's identity as a communicator is essential to good preaching. I usually begin by telling students in the first homiletics class to take a good look at themselves and how they relate to others. Self-knowledge and personal scrutiny are the beginning of wisdom in preaching and communicating.

Scrutinizing Personal Communication

I ask students to be particularly conscious, as the week passes, of how they meet and talk to people, how they relate to friends, acquaintances, strangers and people who come in and out of their lives fleetingly and casually. Other communicating areas I focus on are the ways they tell a story or re-create an event in their life for others. Ask yourself these questions: Can I tell a story or re-create an event in my life with emotional feeling that will help someone else capture some of that moment? Can you use image words and concrete language in your speech, or do you live in a world of cerebral language and theory? Do you mask your feelings with headiness, evasiveness or over-intellectualizing? Are you always aware of being in control of your speech and emotions, with the result that authentic enthusiasm and naturalness of expression are blocked out?

Some of these questions are given to the students to try out during the next week. In the area of meeting people they are to ask themselves: Am I comfortable in meeting people? Am I comfortable in introducing myself to people? Do I keep my eyes down when I'm talking to others? Are my hands in my pocket? Do I avoid introducing myself to people? Do I walk away as soon as I can from groups or newly introduced people?

How do I shake hands? With vigor, or as if I were holding a dead fish? Is there energy in my communication with others? Is there enthusiasm? What gets me excited? Is it football? Is it baseball? Do I like to tell jokes and stories? Do I ever get excited about sharing a faith experience? Do I want to talk about what I'm doing in ministry? Am I different in my interest and energy level when I'm on a one-to-one basis or within small groups than I am in public? Am I the type of person who will yell and jump and cheer and boo and curse with vigor as a spectator, but become placid, passive and unenthused when I'm in the pulpit or talking about faith or ministry?

Answers to some of these questions will give clues to your own expertise as a communicator. Other questions relate to your body image. How do you experience your body? Are you self-conscious? How do you walk? Are you stooped over? Do you drag your feet? Do you speak with gestures? Is there a range of feeling and emotion in your language? Are you comfortable with your appearance? What is your self-image like? Do you like yourself? Do you respect yourself? This all has to do with ego strength—and is a good part of quality speaking. Are you embarrassed by your size? Do you feel you are too tall, too short, too fat or too thin? If so, what have you done about it, or are you doing now?

Christianity is a religion which believes that God became a man. His body was the point of mediation between us and God the Father. We saw him with our eyes. We felt him. He touched us. He walked with us. We saw his compassion and his anger. He fed us bread and wine. God's word took flesh and lived among us. God used a body to make his spirit known. "If I could only touch his cloak, I would be healed."

More questions come into our exegesis of self as a communicating person. How do you use humor? Is it at another's expense? Do you feel that you have a genuine sense of humor or is your every attempt contrived? Is your humor crude? Does it elevate people and make them feel good? Does your humor have a sense of irony or is it cynical? Humor, in or out of the pulpit, will often reveal your attitude toward people, and this can make its way into pulpit signs and signals which positively or negatively affect your preaching. Unfortunately, there are priests who try always to be funny in the pulpit. Their humor is an attempt to hide a lot of things: lack of preparation, discomfort with sharing their faith, a need for attention, or immaturity. Whatever it is, it quickly leads to boredom, and the congregation sizes up this kind of preacher as not worth listening to. It erodes faith and breeds cynicism on the part of the faithful.

Sharing Your Faith: Relationships

In the sphere of emotions, the good preacher will be able to reflect with some ease on his own feelings and thoughts, fears, likes, dislikes, hopes and joys with others in such a way that he invites them to do the same. Can you, without embarrassment, help others to feel the presence of God in their own lives? Can you invite them into your faith experiences, speak of your beliefs without being righteous and pietistic? Can you speak comfortably about God, Jesus, the saints, Scripture, and how God has touched you in your own life? Do you avoid projecting yourself in the pulpit as a religious person, seeking rather to be a "good Joe"—anything to prevent people seeing you as a man of faith? Are you comfortable with being a member of the Catholic or Protestant Church or of the Synagogue?

What about your personal relationships? Are these relationships healing and reconciling? Do you stir up trouble, hold grudges, forgive but never forget? Do you keep the pot boiling, spread gossip or breed suspicion? Do your relationships lend themselves to listening and learning from others? Can you affirm someone else's faith, strengths and beliefs? Do you respect others' beliefs when they differ from you own? Can you state your own beliefs without putting another's down?

Questions, questions, questions. They may appear to be like an old examination of conscience, but they are crucial to being a public communicating person. I believe it is important to know and to deal with the way others respond to us when we meet. Do we help to bring them out of themselves? Do we make them comfortable? Are we inviting, hospitable people? Do we take the initiative to put others at ease when we notice them faltering, or do we walk away? Can we sense when people are uncomfortable with us? Do we know why? Can we begin conversations and sustain them, or do we rely on others to seize the initiative and then sustain the pace?

As an exercise in communicating skills, ask a friend to tell you how he or she sees you. Better still, choose someone who isn't a close friend, but who knows and respects you, and ask him or her the same question. Ask how you come across as a person of faith. Do you communicate well? Then, seek ways to strengthen the strong points and lessen the impact of the weak ones.

Vulnerability in the Pulpit

Remember, the pulpit makes us vulnerable. People who see and hear us over a long period of time will see us pretty much as we are. They will know if we're shy, sloppy, casual, unprepared, arrogant or sensitive, whether we're reading the sermon, if we can share our faith comfortably and how important Scripture is to our preaching.

Remember, too, that preaching does not magically transform the preacher into a different kind of person. People will quickly catch on to ministerial persons to whom announcing the word of God is but a casual, passing interest. They will know who can speak with conviction about faith—and they will expect it. They want their flesh and blood ministers to tell them effectively about Jesus Christ, about God and about faith. They want, and need, the priest to perfect his talents and to discipline himself in preaching so that they who sit in the pews will be fed bread and not stone.

Closely united to preaching is the manner in which a priest says Mass. Celebrating the liturgy is an act of communication. People size up the priest at the altar, too. Is he casual? Sloppy? What's his contact with the people? Does he appear as if this act of worship is a private affair between him and God? With increasing frequency, preaching courses and workshops help the priest to observe himself in the important communicative act of celebrating Mass and developing sound skills in order that prayerful contact is made between him and the people. The altar and pulpit cannot be separated in your role as a communicating public church person.

The area of relationships is important to good communication. Jesus himself struggled to effect relationships to work his Father's will. He ran away from the crowds at times, but they pursued him. It is evident that the whole of the New Testament is a gathering of stories in which Jesus is engaged in a relationship with someone. There is conflict, dynamism, engagement of people and ideas. The Sermon on the Mount is a blueprint for personal relationships transformed by faith: turn the other cheek, forgive your enemies, purify your heart. No one could ever say that Jesus was bland or unenthusiastic. He was a supreme communicator—at one with his Father, working to reveal his Father's will to others. When Jesus listened to people, healed them, talked to them, forgave them, called their values to judgment, offered new ways to follow, told parables, fed, calmed, consoled, exorcised and raised the dead—this took energy out of him. "I feel that power has gone out of me," he said when the woman touched the hem of his garment. Faith produced energy and engagement.

Scripture tells us that Jesus grew in age, wisdom and grace before beginning his public ministry. He did not possess all his gifts at once. So, too, with preaching and proclamation. This essential gift for evangelization and renewal grows in skill, ability, wisdom and grace.

Faith as Key to Proclamation: Personal Exegesis

A critique of oneself as a communicating person finally extends to an exegesis of one's own spiritual and religious life. Good preaching requires continual self-scrutiny. One's life is to be probed. Do I personally have a lively sense of God's presence? Do I experience the good news of Jesus in my own life? Where and in whom and in what kind of persons and events do I experience the healing and forgiving presence of Jesus? What is it about my personal faith that excites me to share it with others? Do I hear my own voice rather than God's? In what, whom and where does my own sin consist? Can I identify with key persons of Scripture such as Abraham, Isaiah, Ezekiel, Jonah, Jeremiah, Moses and the people of Israel? Do I perhaps see myself in Peter's boyish impetuousness, his vulnerability and his openness? Or is it in Mary's simple trust, her fear, her questions, or her fidelity? Can I join my belief to that of the crowds who trusted that Jesus could feed them on what appeared to be so little in the abundance of life and grace even when it seemed all used up?

All of these questions which probe our own faith and signal our capacity to see the biblical world as a present world—now, not "back there"—add depth to preaching. Their experiences, though lived in different times and places, are also the experiences of people in the pews before you.

This exegesis of your own life will help you to understand those people in the pews. Individuals ask similar and identical questions. Their questions and yours will help keep your preaching anchored in Scripture and in life's real issues. Their faith and the questions which probe your own life will guard against your succumbing to theological-philosophical language and treatises that have little to do with concrete moments of people's lives. Such probing will protect your preaching from becoming an ego trip. This honest examination of your life and faith, this self-exegesis, will keep you close to the people and help you to realize what all good preaching starts from: an acceptance of oneself as a sinner who stands equal with all mankind before God, gifted by his grace and given the strength to proclaim his saving deeds to all who can hear.

Schooled in Scripture

A religious sister who team-taught a preaching course with me says: "Preachers should always go to school in the Scriptures and in the liturgy." Both Scripture and liturgy are a proclamation that God is near to us—in word, sacrament, symbol, and ritual, and in one another, gathered as the worshiping community of faith. She insisted that we keep reminding ourselves that God *always* works in and through the Scriptures. We *may,* in fact, find him on the golf course, or at dinner with someone charming and chic, or in Kahlil Gibran or Simon and Garfunkel, because God will not be shackled by anything or anyone. We know *for certain,* however, that he is always working in Scripture. "Use the Scriptures," my sister friend would say. "Become steeped in them and you won't go wrong in preaching."

And the people will not go wrong in you.

Sized-Up Pastorally

Good preaching invites persons to seek further pastoral care from the preacher. Often a person will come to the rectory asking for a specific priest because that person has made a positive decision about the priest by observing him celebrate Mass or by listening to him preach. "I figured he would be understanding from what he said in his sermon, or by the way he prayed the Mass," is one observation. No other space or place in the church so exposes the priest as a public person as does the pulpit and altar. The great majority of people have only those few minutes on Sunday to decide what kind of person the priest is—by the way he speaks to them, by the attitude he communicates toward the sacred event of proclamation and eucharistic celebration, by his words, gestures, stories, and demeanor, whether he is brusque, caring, sloppy, casual, scolding, inviting, reasonable, kind, open or challenging. Remember that the preaching moment is *the great pastoral moment* of the week for most people. The congregation's decision about you is most often made right there, for better or for worse. Why not prepare then, with your whole heart and mind and soul, for that moment?

This emphasis on the personal demeanor and character of the preacher is centuries old. Aristotle spoke of it, as did Augustine. If that demeanor and character are looked upon favorably, Augustine said, that will cause the congregation to have a feeling of "friendliness and attentiveness toward the preacher, more than style, rhetoric, brilliance or doctrine." I like to think that Augustine had in mind this exegesis of one's life when he said that the congregation "ceases to listen with submission to a man who does not listen to himself, and in despising the preacher they learn to despise the word that is preached."

Augustine believed that the image or estimate which the congregation has of the preacher as a person has an important bearing on his persuasiveness. The preacher, he said, must project himself as a person of "competence, good character, good will. . . . " The preacher communicates to his congregation to the extent to which he possesses these attributes through his choice of sermon content. Arrangement of material, use of language, personal projection and manner of delivery are all essentials of good preaching. "What the preacher is and does before and during the actual preaching moment," Augustine said, "has an influence on his personal preaching success."

It is impossible to hyperbolize the importance of the spiritual character in a person who is ordained to preach the word of God. That does not mean that a sinful man should not preach. If that were so, pulpits would be covered with cobwebs. We begin preaching with an interior confession of sinfulness coupled with a promise to sound out the depths of Scripture as often as possible. We open our hearts to God's saving grace, trying to know ourselves without delusion. Often overlooked by many ministers of the word are the very sources of the listeners' *impressions* of the preacher's character which they derive from his communication skills, delivery and content. A badly delivered sermon, a consistent proclamation that is devoid of content, enthusiasm and preparation and sloppily delivered, easily conveys to the person in the pew the idea: "Father doesn't care, and he doesn't respect me." When he doesn't care about the word (at least that's what it sounds like), "will he care about other things in his ministry?" If the word of the Lord, that precious ointment of salvation, is so casually borne, how will what seem to be lesser things of faith be met by this same minister?

When I related all of this on one occasion to a homiletics class, one student responded by saying: "People don't want phonies in the pulpit, and all this communications stuff is merely frosting on the cake." He added: "It seems that all this stuff about presence, projection and proclamation is confusing drama and acting with sacred science and God's grace."

My personal response is to say that there is not much danger of that confusion taking place. The preacher cannot continually express himself publicly without revealing who and what he is. Most of us are essentially the person inside as we seem on the outside. What the preacher reveals, however, will determine whether or not he is to be believed. All that he has said, from posture to projection, energy to enthusiasm and preparation to proclamation, will contribute to his effectiveness. He is a preacher who has been called by God to use his own personality in its fullness, and at its best, as a vehicle to speak his truth. Using skill honed by discipline and reflection is a virtue, and it would be unseemly even to consider that perfection in the preaching discipline is a sellout to authenticity. God's grace does not normally work miracles in the preacher.

Reflection on the Week's Events

Lastly, in this critique of self as a communicating person, some attention should be given to reflection on the past week's events. How have they affected me personally? What questions of faith have they raised to me? What stumbling blocks have they put in the way of myself as a believing person? What doubts have they cast on my belief in the nearness of God? What news events have affected me? What pastoral moments have been important? Will anything that has happened to me this week cause me to project feelings into my sermon which may do damage to the faith and unity of the Church? For example, will my disagreement with the bishop this week trickle its anger into my sermon? Will my falling out with the pastor affect my attitude toward authority in the Church? If so, it would be better not to preach about religious authority this week. What are my relationships like to those close to me: family, friends? If everything has gone wrong and I have fallen flat on my face most of the time this week in my pastoring efforts, that fact may alter my optimism about my competence in general. When sickness, such as the flu, has kept me down most of the week, and I know fairly certain that Sunday will greet me unrecovered, I had better plan for a less bold pulpit endeavor.

This is all part of the preacher knowing himself. It's all part of tracing his footsteps over the past week through the brier patches to find out where his bruises are so he won't project his anger or disillusionment onto the people. This calls for prayer and reflection, getting in touch with himself, some particular examen leading to self-knowledge, all of which will ultimately become strength for the pastoral moment of preaching.

When I prepare a homily several days in advance for Sunday, I try to estimate my energy level for that day. For example, two weddings on Saturday, an evening wake, and several known stress situations during the week on into Saturday will clue me in on my physical state for Sunday. Will I be tired? Is there any space for me to rest and reflect before Sunday? Perhaps I should settle for a shorter homily, that is, one that requires less strain on delivery. Obviously, the time, content, the level of physical output will all be shaped by knowledge of what the week looks like in advance or retrospect. A full week's schedule, never interrupted, in which preaching preparation gets short shrift is a danger signal to pastoral ministry. "Workaholism," as an excuse for lack of preparation, is a vicious circle. A busy schedule from Monday to Sunday, with no time to prepare a homily, could evoke the feeling: "Oh well, I can't be doing the Lord's work and at the same time be putting aside several hours a week for preaching preparation. People won't be served."

Much could be said about this attitude. Suffice it to say that very few pastoral problems of a one-to-one nature will go unsolved, even when the priest announces to his congregation that Wednesday or Thursday is sacrosanct for preaching preparation. People will respect that. They will also find other times to see you and the mission of the Church will be better served. The few people whom you may have seen (and doubtlessly will see) are only a handful compared to the several hundreds you can reach on Sunday through the preaching event as pastoral moment.

Exegesis of oneself, learning the self-wisdom of which Augustine speaks, will give insight into personal hang-ups which are bound to affect my preaching. What are my prejudices? What irks me? Pet peeves? Hang-ups about sex, women, children? A misogynist is unlikely to treat pastorally and sensitively the controversial subject of women in ministry. A priest who spends nearly all of his time with teenagers and rarely ever with adults is likely to relate poorly to adults. It might well temper the way he sees the world of adults and speaks to their situation. If marriage and a family are seen as a "drag" or a second-best vocation, that also might color homilies at weddings. A priest who is annoyed by children had best stay away from preaching to children. The more insights one has into himself, the better he will be able to preach. The ideal pastoral situation, of course, is to have a ministerial person who can rise to any occasion like St. Paul who wrote: "To the Greeks, I am a Greek, to the Gentiles, a Gentile. . . . I am all things to all men." The more universal our talents and interests, the more openness we have to events, cultures, people and groups in society, and the more ways God can use us as his instrument.

Conclusion

"It is the Spirit who strengthens in all things. . . . "

After a preacher has considered all of these things (and hopefully during his probing and pondering) he must, like any child of God, put his trust in the Holy Spirit. It is he who strengthens us in all things. It has been helpful to me, on a number of occasions, to pray with those involved in the liturgy, just before the service begins, a prayer that tries to put all labor and human skill into proper perspective, asking the Spirit to stand beside me and in me while preaching God's word. Ultimately, it is to know that my faith rests not on the wisdom of men but on the foolishness of God, and a radical belief, too, that when I've done my part, God will put words in my mouth.

The constant and perennial faith and tradition of the Church gives us some assurance that God smiles broadly on our efforts.

SPECIFIC POINTS AND EXERCISES FOR STUDY

From POINTS FOR PREPARATION AND DELIVERY (See *Introduction* I)

I. Make initial check:
   (a) Review next week's schedule. Is it heavy? What will Saturday be like: How are you feeling emotionally? Physically? Block out three or four hours for preparation.
   (b) World events, TV shows. Try to get a sense of what media or world events might shape the attitudes of your congregation during the week.

II. Pick out an object in the room and write a paragraph describing it in detail so that a reader could clearly visualize what it looks like. Next, take an emotional feeling and write about it in detail. Describe it, in writing, for someone else to read. Then, with the words in front of you on paper, practice communicating the feeling *as if* it were spontaneous and unwritten.

III. Take some of the questions in this chapter (scrutinizing personal communication and speech) and jot down one- or two-line answers for yourself.

IV. List five to ten personal strengths which you feel would help you to be a good preacher. List three to five areas you would like to strengthen in order to improve your personal communication skills and preaching.

From EXERCISES AND REFLECTIONS TO ENHANCE PREACHING (See *Introduction* II)

I. Use body language. Be aware, during the week, of the ways in which you walk, sit, and talk. These can be clues to the kind of communicating person you are: involved? distant? impersonal? lethargic? enthusiastic? dynamic? passive? uninterested? What about your tone of voice, pitch, resonance, rate, rhythm, personal appearance, clothing? What signals are you picking up from people with whom you relate during the week? Involvement? Avoidance? Are you active and involved or reclusive and withdrawn?

3.
Exegesis: Biblical and Personal

"In Scripture, divine things are handed to us in the way in which men are accustomed."

St. Thomas Aquinas

"God's words are expressed in human language . . . like man's word in every way except for error."

St. John Chrysostom

"The Lord stood by my side and gave me strength so that through me the preaching task might be completed and all nations might hear the Gospel."

2 Tim. 4:17

The commitment to exegete a Scripture passage is a commitment to both scholarship and to research. The exegete takes a journey into the mind, culture, people, land, language and intention of the biblical writer. When one embarks on this journey, he leaves our busy world and becomes, for a while at least, a wayfarer in a strange land.

Exegesis helps me to feel that I am in touch with the people and culture to whom the biblical word was personally addressed. It enriches my own understanding of the perennial truth of revelation. Exegesis can be a special moment of prayerful reflection on the proclamation event for the preacher and congregation alike.

What did the author mean when he wrote this? Why did he use

this word and not another? What was the mood of life then? What did the writer intend to plant in the mind of the listener?

To answer these questions is the homilist's task. The preacher must engage the words and be able to point out the relevance and meaning of the text to his contemporary listener. Preaching is to be solidly founded in a decision about the pastoral situation found in the meaning of the text in question, along with an understanding of the limits of the passage.

When we read Scripture, we understand very quickly how both our culture and our mind-set can be vastly different from that of the author of the Scripture text as well as of the people who heard it proclaimed. Faith, language, culture, religious beliefs and customs shaped those original texts. Exegesis helps us to preserve the wholeness of the scriptural message. It takes us on a journey into the biblical world with such guides as poetry, allegory, parable, myth, biography, drama, history, metaphor, folk tales and proverbs. Time, place, and customs may change. Man's search for God does not. He still feels blind, lame, deaf, in need of forgiveness, in need of healing and hope.

Exegesis as Corrective

Exegesis is essential. It *must* be the source and guide for all preaching. How many times have you heard a preacher follow his reading of the Gospel with the thought: "What did St. Matthew mean by these words? *Precisely* this." He then goes on to tell you "precisely" what *he* interprets it to mean. One priest, on the feast of the Assumption, read all sorts of things into the texts, totally unsupported either by exegesis or tradition. Yet he somehow told the congregation "exactly" what Luke had in mind.

Exegesis will counter the temptation of the preacher to think that he knows "precisely" what the inspired writer of Scripture meant. Every preacher stands in danger of communicating his own conception of things. The Scriptures, like the teachings of the Church, prove a stimulant to our thought and meditation, and the product of that thought can be satisfying. But to the degree that it is our application to, or conclusion from, the Scriptures, to that degree, it is not God's own word. The congregation may be inspired and impressed with the fruits of our own reflections, and may even profit in their lives from it, but in our role as preacher—or teacher—it is more important (even imperative) to make clear to our hearers "precisely" what the sacred writer hears God himself saying.

Pope Pius XII on the Need for Exegesis

Pope Pius XII cautioned against such dangers as preachers proposing Scripture interpretations of their own. While he admitted that some accommodation may be made to a "spiritual" sense, he pointed out that it must always be done with "moderation and restraint." The "faithful," especially those educated in sacred and secular sciences, "want to know what God himself has expressed to us in the sacred writings, rather than what some capable speaker or writer may be able to express by a dexterous use of the Bible's words."

"The word of God," he continued, "living, powerful and sharper than any two-edged sword, reaches even to the division of soul and spirit and joints and marrow, and discerns the thoughts and intentions of the heart. This word has no need of human embellishment or accommodation to strike and move minds. The sacred pages, composed under the inspiration of God's Spirit, abound with a meaning of their own. They have a power of their own."

Exegesis: A Commitment to Research

Since the purpose of exegesis is to discover and "expound the true meaning of the sacred books," the process is a commitment to time, research, comparison of texts, sorting and sifting, resolving conflicts among translations and appreciating various interpretations of Scripture scholars. Without exegesis, a preacher listens to himself and is in danger of simply talking "off the top of his head" about the meaning of biblical texts. The pulpit becomes a private preserve for his own pet theories and interpretations. Preaching without exegesis is an affront to the sacred character of God's revealing word. It quickly leads to biblicism.

The preacher's task is to discover the true meaning of the revealed word as the Spirit of God guided the scribe who wrote the words. His task is to capture the meaning and sense of the passage—

the literal sense (what the human author intended to express and *did* express). This sense was born out of a concrete time, place and experience. A pastoral concern at the time often determined the construction of a story. The Church's reflection on the Scriptures over the centuries has shed light on the meaning and ways that the text has been accommodated to a specific need in the Church. Certain emphases, texts and words were responses of the Church to pastoral problems within a young and struggling Christian community. Frequently, during exegesis, the preacher will find that the same pastoral problems exist today, in the same or another form. Thus, the intended meaning of the passage by the writer throws light on our own present darkness. The same passage speaks to the same faith problems in different ages.

Exegesis Gives Meaning of Texts

When the preacher reads Scripture, obviously many meanings come to mind. We may see real or symbolic meanings unintended by the author. Over the years the Church and commentators gave meanings to passages which have been "traditioned" down. Some have been accommodated for purposes of Church or personal piety. These meanings may never have been intended by the biblical author. Exegesis give the preacher a clue as to the context out of which the Scripture passage was first proclaimed and addressed to the pastoral needs of that day. Exegesis tips you off as to why Jesus or the evangelist used certain words or events as examples. It also guards against "isogesis"—reading into and imposing on Scripture what is not there.

More than once I have heard preachers use the text describing the finding of the child Jesus in the temple as justification for preaching obedience to parents and authority. These preachers go far beyond any meaning intended by the writer. Good exegesis would have given some hint that such a personal interpretation was intellectually uncritical and without foundation either in revelation or Church tradition, to say nothing of the obvious injustice to the congregation—especially to disobedient children.

The preacher's responsibility to include the meaning of the text in his remarks does not suggest that he involve his listener in all the scientific and technical details of exegesis. This is not preaching. It is the preacher's task to interpret the meaning for the people according to the circumstances of their lives. The preacher's true concern is to reflect on the Scripture passage and to critically evaluate it through exegetical scholarship. He then pieces out a meaning which says something to the congregation about the way in which God has spoken through this recorded event.

Most preachers are not professional exegetes, but their courses in Scripture give enough instruction and experience so that they will know where they may go for help in interpreting the Scriptures for homiletic use. Exegesis will help the preacher to narrow down certain topics for preaching purposes. It will give him an idea for a sermon which reflects the integrity of the passage. Exegesis will help him to discover other meanings which appear in the passage. It will help him in his own understanding of the passage even where he does not share all this information with his congregation. The preacher will, with a context of meaning derived from exegesis, emphasize the intent of the writer rather than focus on an isolated word which may not, in fact, have been the intention of the writer at all.

Example: Matthew's Text on Divorce

We might consider here Matthew's text on divorce. Exegesis of that passage informs the preacher that it is not to be interpreted solely as a facile condemnation of divorce to justify, absolutely, the Church's prohibition as we now know it. Rather, Jesus' statement considers many aspects of Jewish law regarding marriage and putting one's wife away. One can only understand this text in the light of Jewish customs and laws found in the Old Testament Books of Deuteronomy and Leviticus, which relate to the inferior status of women in that society and the responsibilities of wives to their husbands, according to Jewish law. Exegesis saves the preacher from insensitive and dogmatic overkill. Exegesis guards against meanings which, though valid from Canon Law and its application, may not have been the sole intention of the author. To have exegeted the Matthew passage with concern for the meaning that divorce has in that culture could lead a preacher toward deeper pastoral concern from the pulpit toward those suffering marital separation.

Take another example. In John 6:22–29 Jesus is speaking about "bread." In the early verses he refers to "perishable food," and opposes it to "eternal food." A quick exegesis reveals that Jesus is using bread and food metaphorically. Food, in the second part of the metaphor, means "doctrine." The Jews understand "bread" to be equal to "Torah." To know this simple fact makes it much easier to preach on this passage and to help the listener understand what Jesus is talking about.

Exegesis Clarifies and Familiarizes

History, culture, religious contexts, the practices of the people, morality, cults, apparent contradiction between and among various biblical texts, why two evangelists omit or vary details of the same story—all of this knowledge will come through exegesis and strengthen the serious preacher's hand in presenting revelation through preaching. Good exegesis will help the preacher to point out the relevance of the Gospel message today to the lives of the congregation, their faith and their questions. Exegesis makes vital and new what is old.

For preachers and would-be preachers whose education in Scripture has been deficient, there continue to be encouraging signs. Biblical institutes are held periodically around the country. Articles and books on preaching are beginning to appear, and popular works of Scripture abound, solidly based in scholarship. Commentaries, such as the *Jerome Biblical Commentary,* are treasure houses for the preacher committed to preparation. Persons who preach might subscribe to periodicals which give good exegesis of the three cycles of the Lectionary (see the Bibliography for Homily Series and Resources). These will keep the preacher on his exegetical toes in helping to introduce his congregation to the wealth of the revealed word.

Exegesis helps the preacher to become thoroughly familiar with the passage in question. I find it helpful to retell the passage, either alone to myself, or to someone else. This insures that I at least know the story without having to read it. I listen to myself in order to know that I am using words which make sense to me. Most important, too, is to reread the passages immediately previous to and following the one being used for preaching. Often the texts used in the liturgy are taken out of a larger context and their meaning is more fully amplified by an event, a circumstance or a saying of Jesus cited immediately prior to the text used for the sermon. A prior passage might give a clue into reasons why Jesus said something, or reacted in a certain way. It might explain his exasperation with the people, the kind of town he has just visited, what happened there, what Jesus has just said or done, or what influences the people whom he has met. These few moments of reading the passages at both ends of your text will enliven the meaning of your sermon. You might even want to refer to the previous passage in your sermon to help the congregation understand the context of your own remarks.

Exegesis and Personal Reflection

In exegesis, I feel that it is most important for the preacher to spend time meditating on how the passage reflects his own life. Many questions pose themselves: What are the times in my own life when I feel like the blind man? What must it be like to be physically and/or spiritually blind? What circumstances in my situation and life are similar? What circumstances are different? How is my culture different and/or the same? How is authority used here?

And further: What are the blindnesses, the prejudices for which I need forgiveness? Where do I need to see more clearly in my faith? When, like Lazarus, have I felt bound in wrapping cloths, as if dead, and someone's understanding or compassion called me back into life? What are my hungers, thirsts and fears? When, as in the multiplication of the loaves and the fishes, have I been given something I thought was not there?

Who and what kind of people are in the Gospel story? Who peoples the Old Testament passage? What are these people like? How do they speak? What words do they use? How do I think they felt? How would I feel if I were in the same situation? What feelings does the Scripture writer place in his characters? Is it fear, frustration, anxiety or expectation? Is it joy, fulfillment or hope? Can I identify with any of them?

What characterizes the conversation taking place between or among various figures in the story, particularly between Jesus and other persons? What is Jesus' reaction to different kinds of personality types? What is his response to authority people? How does he feel about persons who are down-and-out, or toward sin? What are his emotions and his solutions to human problems? What does the conversation in the passage reveal about the person's life, his faith and his hopes? Are these the same as mine or yours? With what biblical characters do you identify most strongly? What are their traits? What is the quality of their faith or their fears? Which ones would you like to be if that were possible?

Imagine yourself talking to Jesus. What would you say to him? What do you think he would say to you? How does Jesus engage the people with whom he comes in contact? What questions does he ask of them? Against what sins does he react most strongly? Against what kind of people does he appear harsh? Against what personal and societal sins does Jesus render the strongest judgment? What questions does Jesus ask? How does Jesus respond when the people either reject him or fail to accept him or understand what he is saying? What human trait angers Jesus more than others? Is it adultery? Is it self-righteousness? Or is it pride or lack of forgiveness or legalism, or failure to defend the poor?

Exegesis Keeps Jesus Rooted in Church Tradition

This kind of exegesis will help the preacher to focus on real people like us. It will sharpen the images of human situations out of which the story was written. These personal questions and creative meanderings keep Jesus real for all of us. Our pulpit words are to be checked against the shaping of Jesus into a theological or philosophical abstraction. Sermons reflect the dynamism of a living, breathing and feeling person with whom we can in some way identify. Exegesis checks tendencies to turn Jesus into a disembodied and abstract spirit. Joining these questions to serious exegesis will prevent us from putting Jesus into our own pre-conceived categories where we present him in some narrow, simple slot, such as judge, "just a man," morality giver, or "do-gooder."

During the excessive personalism of the 1960's many preachers painted their own Jesus—a Jesus who often came off like a "teddy bear," devoid of all feeling except a warm, cuddly love. Preachers lost touch with the rich, Hebrew tradition of Jesus. Instead Jesus was

used to justify every humanist impulse. For some, he was only a social activist, an angry, righteous judge against the established order.
For others, he was just a wonderful man, the most perfect man who
ever lived, who came to teach us how to love. For others still, Jesus
was the morality giver who told us what we could and could not do.
And still others saw Jesus as okaying anything, so long as one felt it
was good. Jesus ran the gamut of personalities; most of them, however, were constructions and projections of those who created their
own Jesus, with little or no scholarly exegesis to root that understanding in the living tradition of the Church out of which the sacred
writings grew.

Exegesis also helps us to understand the meaning of demons,
evil, angels and miracles in the religious and social culture in which
Jesus lived. Good exegesis will guard against cultic interpretations
which often lead to bizarre religious behavior. Study of the exegete
will help to resolve apparent contradictions in the Gospels. John, for
example, shows Jesus as loving the world and hating the world. He
condemns the world, but he gives his life for the world. Reflection on
John through the eyes of the exegete will dispel any notion that Jesus
is clear-cut in his attitude toward the world. That attitude should, in
some way, be reflected in our sermon and will check tendencies toward tangents and tirades about the "evil world"—a favorite pas-
time, incidentally, of some preachers.

Shared Reflection

Finally, in the exegesis step of preparation, I would include,
when possible, some formal period of reflection on the readings with
a fellow priest, layperson or friend—anyone who might like to do
this. These discussions can boost one's understanding of the Scriptures. The Holy Spirit inspires each of us according to our own gifts,
strengths, limitations and experiences. Another person's reflection
on the resurrection may, in fact, trigger a memory of an experience
which was salvific in our own lives. His own shared reflection may
recall an event in which we experienced God raising us up from our
own feelings of deadness. A searching of common themes, a pooling
of ideas, insights and inspiration, can strengthen our belief that the
Holy Spirit works in and through the community of believers. We

understand then that your faith strengthens mine, and mine strengthens yours.

Whenever I have combined the reflection of others to my own exegesis, I have come away richer. People have seen into the passage in a way I had not thought possible, and their reflections shape whole new ways for me to look at biblical events. Discussion of the text helps ideas and insights to germinate and to grow, allowing the text to become more a part of me. It opens up possibilities not there before. Especially prior to liturgy, planning groups can spend time exegeting the passages together, meditate on them and then share their understanding. For the major liturgical feasts of Holy Week, for Sunday liturgies, and for special days such as Thanksgiving, it is not uncommon for planning groups to spend several hours together reading the text and meditating. A discussion follows in which people freely share their insights. The group gets together one or more times to narrow down themes for the sermon. After everyone exegetes the passage, together they discuss the exegete's understanding of the passage in relation to the culture and the faith questions of that time, and they reflect on the meaning for the contemporary scene. When we do this, we let the text possess and make a claim on each of us. We do not choose a text to ratify our pre-conceived notions for the liturgy. We stay with the texts offered by the Church's experience and let them confront our situations, then grapple to eke out their meanings for us, here and now, and there and tomorrow.

I once preached at the major Holy Week services of a large city parish, which included: Holy Thursday, the Seven Last Words of Good Friday, the Good Friday Liturgy and all Easter Sunday Masses. I began my preparation early in Lent, reading the Scriptures, thinking about them, jotting down ideas as they came to me, reading various commentaries from books and looking over sermons written on the same passages. I put a note on the bulletin board of my community, inviting anyone who would like to reflect on them with me as helpful preparation. Two persons responded. We spent about five hours total in sharing insights.

Following that, I met with a professor of biblical studies—one especially respected for her pastoral application of the Scriptures—and together we discussed each text, shared ideas, exchanged images, discussed the complexity of the congregation, and reflected on our concern over what unique problems existed in their city. We took the Seven Last Words and focused on themes or human experiences of our own—and of others—which related to such words as thirst, forgiveness, feelings of abandonment, and mother and what it means to "commend" oneself to another. We kept asking: "What will this passage say to this congregation"—a very mixed one in age, background, education and social status. I kept thinking how I could try to reach all of them by attaching some universal meaning reflected in the Seven Last Words of Christ. This process, combined with exegesis, greatly lightened my burden, converted it into prayer and made my preaching a much deeper religious experience. It also opened up exciting possibilities for preaching the word. Some in-depth discussion had preceded the preaching, and so the texts became part of me. I had digested them. Shared reflection lets us know that we are not alone in the task we have undertaken. God's word comes to us powerfully as a community of believers—not as isolated, lonely souls groping alone in the dark hoping to find God in our lives.

Homily Services: But Beware!

The would-be preacher may want to check on some homily services. I am reluctant to admit this as a preparation aid, especially in the early days of preaching, if only because our weak human nature settles for the easy path to proclamation. Preaching preparation requires discipline because it is a difficult, time-consuming effort. St. Thomas might have called it the "bonum arduum"—the "difficult good." It is too easy to settle into the habit of canned homilies, to take someone else's ideas, doctor them up a bit and present them as one's own. The preacher who does this on a weekly basis is in danger of living a shallow faith life. Little religious growth takes place in a person who settles for this method. Homily services can put up a barrier to prevent the congregation from ever hearing the preacher share his own personal faith.

Unless a preacher is highly skilled in his own right, it usually will become apparent to the listener that the preacher has settled for someone else's work. An astute congregation will size up a priest's preaching ability from having observed him pastorally and liturgically and in talking with him privately. Knowing him as a person outside of the pulpit clues them in to the kind of communicating person he is. Some preachers read their sermons—and they read badly. Some preachers read good sermons badly. Often, however, they read, even more ineffectively, the sermons belonging to someone else. A safe assumption is that a sermon must come from a person's heart; it must be his own faith that is shared. It may be someone else's ideas, shared together, or someone else's faith that has shaped his own, but ultimately, when the sermon is given, this faith must have been assimilated, digested and owned by the preacher himself. Homily services, when offering an idea or two, can be helpful in presenting anecdotes, stories, and insights into exegesis which can be used in preparation. They should be used, however, only as *one* of many aids, not as substitutes for hard work and research and one's own faith. Some homily series outline the Scriptures well. They've already done the exegesis for you. I have personally found many homily series much too oriented toward humanism, with little reference, except in passing, to the Scripture of the day. Some of these series are written by persons trying too hard to be relevant to every passing issue. Some take the Scriptures seriously and are good. Much, I suppose, depends on personal preference. I usually settle for my own reflections and faith experience as the best possible choice.

When the preacher uses homily services, it is preferable that he say so. There is nothing wrong in using them, so there is nothing wrong in letting the congregation know you use them. A preacher might say, for example, that he found an interesting story or idea in a homily service he read. After telling the story (hopefully he recounts it well), he then develops his own faith expression, ideas, experience, and conclusions with the story as a basis. A preacher often takes the idea of another person (that's why I talked about shared preparation) but brings his own experience to it and develops a powerful faith message for his listener. However, in doing so, the message must be his own. His own words have to shape the final product and his own words have to tell the congregation why *he,* personally, was moved by the other person's experience of God, and was moved to share it.

This reminds me of a story of a terribly embarrassing moment in the early years of my priestly ministry. A homily service sermon struck my fancy. I doctored it up here and there, practiced it until it became part of me, retyped it into deliverable fashion and proclaimed the message with gusto and conviction. I was, fortunately, able to identify with its message in a personal way.

The congregation numbered about three hundred college students, a few neighborhood campus people, and faculty. They liked it, and I was happy as a lark and proud that I had pulled this off. The congregation sat in rapt attention. The homily service had developed a fascinating approach to a particular Gospel story and I had enlarged upon it.

As I was greeting the people after Mass, a young lady approached and said: "Father, may I ask you a personal question?"

"Sure," I said.

"Well, it's about your sermon. Was it your own idea?"

I felt my heart sink. "Foiled by the devil," I thought. I had been caught. I couldn't get out of this one, so I decided to be honest.

"No," I said, "I took it from a homily service and made a few modifications on it."

"Well," she responded, "I was really distracted during it because last weekend at our home parish my pastor gave the exact same sermon. It seemed as though he was reading it word for word. You had more enthusiasm and it sounded more like your own, but it was the same idea and material. It was a weird feeling sitting there knowing I had heard someone else two hundred miles away give the same sermon a week before."

That cured me forever. What was more humiliating was the fact that she asked me the question in the presence of about ten people who were standing around!

The same happened in reverse to me as I listened to a sermon about what our attitude toward the poor should be. It was a strong, prophetic kind of sermon, but I kept feeling that the content somehow did not square with my own perceptions and experience of the priest who was delivering the sermon. It stood in contrast to his usual style, delivery and content. However, I liked what the sermon said.

A day or so later I picked up a magazine, the entire issue of which was devoted to poverty, and there I found, practically word for word, the basic content of the sermon I had heard the day before.

In both instances, my own as a college chaplain, and the second story, it would have been legitimate to say something like this: "I was reading about such and such in this or that magazine and was struck by some of the ideas there. I will build my sermon today around them, joining to my own reflections the insights of the article.

Honesty like this is the best route. Believe me!

Based on both experiences, I've adopted what someone else has said about homily services: "Caution: May Be Habit Forming and Dangerous to Your Growth as a Preacher!"

Conclusion

The means to good preaching are available all around us. Discipline is the key to good preaching. There is no substitute for it. It means setting time aside each week, reflecting on the Scriptures, exegeting from reputable biblical scholars, discussing the Scriptures with others, reading and reflecting on commentaries, writing down notes, writing out the basic ideas of the sermon, practicing alone, and practicing before others (especially if you're in the early stages of developing good preaching habits).

Preaching is the one area of ministry where one has to make some commitment to Pelagianism—working as if all depended on your efforts. Join those efforts to the belief that God uses us as instruments of his grace, and your preaching will open up treasures of faith for those who come to hear.

SPECIFIC POINTS AND EXERCISES FOR STUDY

From POINTS FOR PREPARATION AND DELIVERY (See *Introduction* I)

I. Make initial check:
   (a) Exegete your own life over the past week. What areas of faith, hope, and love emerge as strengths or weaknesses?
   (b) Take the stories, memories, exegesis, and events of the week and reflect on the ways in which God met you in them. Make some of this the focus of your daily and weekly meditation and reflection.
   (c) How do these Scripture passages reflect, similarly, the ways

in which God reveals himself to you today—heals, forgives
you, is your light, raises you up, etc.?

II. Check your presonal library. Make sure you own a few good
biblical commentaries. Check the resources and homily services
listed in the bibliography of this book to familiarize yourself
with them.

III. Keep developing the virtue of trusting biblical commentaries
over personal interpretation of the Scriptures.

IV. For one week, exegete Scripture readings for daily liturgy
whether or not you are going to preach. Take notes; compare
contemporary faith experience with the culture and religious
setting of the Scripture passage.

V. Jot down a few answers to some of the questions in this chapter
under the subhead "Exegesis and Personal Reflection."

From EXERCISES AND REFLECTIONS TO ENHANCE
PREACHING (See *Introduction* II)

I. Read Scripture for fifteen minutes every day. Try to visualize
persons, places, environment of the passage, the inter-relationship of biblical characters with Jesus and each other. Retell out
loud, to yourself, what is happening in the passage. Note, especially in the breviary, the strong image and concrete language of
the psalms, of the prophets, of Jesus. Study the words used.
Write down image words and build up a file on them. Make this
Scripture reading *active* reading.

II. Read aloud a Scripture passage a few times a week. Enunciate
each word clearly and with emphasis to develop a habit of clear
projection, tone and pace. Remember: good speech can be developed through practice.

III. Take a Scripture passage or prose/poetry and go into an auditorium, large church, gymnasium or open field. Shout the passage

to the far corners of the area. This exercise is to develop the habit of audible speech, learning to project loudly enough so that the person in the last pew can hear. It emphasizes "proclamation" over "speaking." But remember: Proclamation is not shouting. Proclamation is a special skill.

4.
Congregation Analysis: Who, What and Where Are My People?

"The Lord knows those who are his."

2 Tim. 2:19

"The preacher should be able to hear his own sermon with the ears of his actual audience."

Karl Rahner

"Father Ed doesn't know where I'm at half the time. If he did, he wouldn't say some of those things from the pulpit. I just can't believe he's sensitive to what I have to put up with in my life."

This is a common complaint. Yet how can the preacher speak to *everyone* in the congregation? Can he reach *all* of the people *all* of the time?

Many studies have been done on audience reaction. The results? The listener is primary. The same principle applies to congregations as to non-religious audiences.

A preacher both flatters and deludes himself when he thinks that everyone is sitting on the edge of the pew wanting to hear what he has to say. If, as some studies indicate, Catholic people have developed low thresholds of listening and expect little of their priests in the pulpit, the preacher had better take seriously what his congregation is thinking.

One thing is clear: the congregation has to *want* to hear what you have to say. The congregation's response grows out of its need to know that what you say will make a difference in their lives. The congregation has rights: the right to hear truth presented with preparation, with enthusiasm, with sensitivity to their lives. They have a right to hear that Jesus is Lord.

The operative words here are "their lives." They are bombarded daily with rock, relativity, doubt, technology and the struggle to make ends meet. Catholics in the pews are caught between two imperatives: man's world and God's kingdom. It's safe to assume that most people think the way their culture does and that they actually enjoy that culture.

The Congregation's Attitudes

Dr. Prentice Meador, a Protestant preacher and writer, says that the modern American congregation brings to church every Sunday several attitudes. It is conformist ("Don't deviate from normal thought patterns, length of sermon or conventional appeals"), sophisticated ("I listen to endless communication and am well informed"), materialistic ("What's in it for me if I accept your point of view?"), respectful of time-saving efficiency ("Stop rambling; get to the point; be efficient in thought, language, organization and time"), searching for personal adjustment ("What does this sermon have to do with me?"), straining for superiority and status ("I believe in excelling. Show me how to improve my life and my family's life"), with respect for progress ("I want movement and progression in your ideas and language") and for universally accepted ideals ("Translate into words so I can understand the ideas of equality, brotherhood, and justice").

Add to these some idols of modern man and you have your congregational mix: "Everything is relative." "Prove it and I'll believe it." "Scientific knowledge is certain; religious knowledge isn't." "After death? Who knows?" " 'Real' means I can touch and see and taste it." "The big things are the great things." "Why change? I can't help being what I am." "Asceticism? Freedom means doing what I like." "Justice? Justice, man, is everybody being equal and doing his own thing." "Put religion first in my life? That's pretentious and arrogant." "What's this about grace? Laws of nature determine everything."

Some or all of these attitudes guide the actions and lives of the Sunday listener. The preacher might think that the people will be intrigued and moved by some event or theme, interesting to the preacher, who prepares and preaches non-stop without ever asking, "Are my ideas touching their concerns? Are they asking the questions I'm answering? Am I in their world?

A preacher who happens to be a professor of chemistry or a photography buff may use the pulpit to share his favorite experiments or to describe his cherished nature scenes—all to raise in his listener's mind questions about God and creation. However, these may not be the questions the congregation is facing this week at home, at work, tending the family, paying the bills, or taking care of a sick parent. The man in the pew may be struggling with: "How can I avoid being caught in my corporation's high-level corruption when I'm part of the decision-making process?" An allusion to chemical experiments or fascinating photography might be a good opener to gain attention, but that is all it should be. The preacher may have decided to preach what he thinks the congregation should hear, but when the congregation isn't interested in hearing his message, the preacher will be up against a brick wall.

"Well," you say, "I can't just preach what people want to hear. A lot of people don't want to hear anything upsetting. They just want a lot of watered-down pablum each week. This congregation doesn't want to hear about helping the poor, about signing petitions to limit the arms race or support nuclear disarmament, or about visiting the sick and the elderly. I refuse to buy into their kind of religion."

Motivating the Congregation

True? *Maybe!* Obviously there are dangers in trying to psyche out the congregation each week, but it's too early to yield on that point. Your task as a preacher is to motivate the congregation. You want to appeal to their faith, which is already there, before you hit them with some hard saying which might turn them off, no matter how valid and biblical and authoritative your message is. The attention of the congregation must never be taken for granted; it must be attracted and held. Your skill as a preacher is on the line. The words of a priest talking about teenagers fit here: "First let them know you care about them. Then they'll listen, and you can do anything with them."

Return for a moment to the priest/chemistry professor. It seems hardly possible that a congregation will appreciate the care of the preacher as a pastoring person when his sermon topic in no way relates to their lives. When the congregation feels that you care for it and are preaching from a stance of wanting it to experience the action of God in their lives, its response will be one of gratitude for the Lord's goodness to them. They will be more likely to respond with faith which praises the Lord—a faith which moves toward conversion. This faith will translate itself into social gospel ministry ("good works") and will change opinions and attitudes on some issues. That is the essence of preaching: to turn one's heart to deeper faith in God's presence and away from narrowness of vision and sinfulness toward new directions and possibilities.

Pastoral "Caring"

When the congregation feels and sees the involvement of the preacher, his sensitivity to their needs and to what's been going on in their lives, they will open their ears and hearts to him. Future sermons will get more attention.

The essence of preaching, like that of all ministry, is founded on caring—"caritas"—love, compassion. The preacher must draw on his own inner life, which he shares by sympathizing with others. When the preacher fails to share the feelings of other persons, he becomes overly introverted and preoccupied with himself. He becomes wrapped up in ideas, theories, concepts and crusades, and forgets the people. This widens the gulf between him and his congregation. Ultimately it creates pessimism both about himself and his ability to reach people, and thus involves the congregation in a vicious circle of discouragement.

The good preacher will study people, get close to them emotionally, and identify with their desire to do good. He will listen to their words and hearts and experience their faith until his understanding and sensitivity toward them is converted into feeling. For example, a preacher may never have been in a hospital or have suffered a serious illness. Somehow, as a caring person, he must move from spectator to direct participant, feeling in his own heart the experiences of the sick. Through participation, he will understand what these persons' feelings are. This will translate into pastoral preaching—into compassion, understanding and sensitivity.

Good and Bad Pastoral Approaches

A student of homiletics was preparing to deliver a homily to the residents of a home for the aged. The diocese had sent out instructions for homily themes to be used over a period of several weeks. This Sunday's theme was on abortion—the right to life—and an outline had been distributed for homiletic use. This young man preached on abortion to a group of old men and women. Except as an academic issue about a social dilemma which, at their age, could hardly be a problem, this misses the mark of pastoral concern.

When asked by the student what the response had been, he said, humorously: "It bombed." He admitted overhearing one old lady say dryly to another, during the coffee hour: "I wish I was young enough to have to make a decision about bearing children." The preacher had failed to preach to their need.

Another example: I attended Mass at a local parish church in the midwest during the week following Pope Paul VI's death. The town was small, and many parishioners were summer residents. The congregation was typical—parents with teenage children, young couples, older people. The priest was an elderly man who came across as warm and gentle. Some of his remarks about Pope Paul, whom he had met some years before, were touching and moving. I sensed warmth in the response of the congregation.

The priest then switched directions. Pope Paul's greatest contribution, he said, was his teaching on birth control. He continued on this tack for quite some time. People were stirring, coughing, thumbing through missalettes. I felt a mixture of emotions, primarily anger and frustration. I thought: "Will he ever end?" The point: whatever is the truth about Pope Paul's contribution, it was hardly the time or place to preach on birth control, an issue which, at the time of the

Pope's encyclical, had split the Church wide open. The occasion of his death was a time to appeal to common grief and to the respect and affection of the people for Pope Paul, a pastoral approach which had marked the beginning of the sermon, but later strayed.

Another example: On Mother's Day, a minister of a rigid fundamentalist sect got up and berated working mothers, denouncing the Equal Rights Amendment, and blaming the high crime rate in the country on families without respect for traditional lines of authority. The sermon was an insult to the people. Whatever may have been factual or true in the sermon fell on rocky ground because the preacher communicated only disdain for the congregation. He missed a great opportunity to reflect, pastorally, on the values of family, the gifts of motherhood, fond memories of generous mothers, and some of the magnificent literature centering on motherhood as a special vocation. He could have won his listeners' hearts and sent them away filled with gratitude and thanksgiving on this Mother's Day.

St. Vincent de Paul had a sound insight when he wrote to tell a young novice: "It is only when the poor *feel* your love that they will forgive you for your gifts of bread."

It is only in knowing that you care for, respect and love your congregation that they will forgive you for presuming that you have something to say about the many ways in which God and believer embrace. When the people feel your love and care, you can expect them to listen even to hard sayings—even to the "no's" which stand in opposition to Christ's Gospel and lead us to a fool's paradise.

Like the poor who allow us to give gifts of bread and remind them of their poverty, the people allow us to preach. It is they, the Church, who publicly commission us, through ordination, and invite us into the pulpit, through the bishop who is their leader. When they feel our concern, see our care, know that we walk where they walk, then they will "forgive" us for calling them to conversion in word and deed.

In Touch with the Congregation

Somehow, the preacher has to be able to express the feelings of the congregation. That is not to say that he merely ratifies what they feel. That would be to lock them into their present attitudes, and all preaching is directed toward a continual conversion experience. It means that the people must feel that you care; they then will extend their hands toward you and ask you to lead them somewhere else: "Take me, by your words, into a deeper faith and sense of God." When what they feel (prejudice, hatred, despair) is seen to be understood by you as a preacher, they will be open to your attempt to convert their hearts. They will open themselves to your dream that life in grace is possible. "Preach to help me grow in the 'fruits of the Spirit.' "

The effective preacher moves inside the congregation's experience. When a preacher begins to think about his future sermon, he visualizes listeners in those pews in front of him and the events of the week in the lives of the people. His business is to deal with the real problems of those people—just as Jesus addressed the real problems of his time. The preacher must think first of them. Instead of writing a sermon and pondering how he will elucidate a particular theme, he should organize it around the people's needs and experiences. He needs what German homileticians call *anknüpfungspunkt*—that point of a sermon in which the preacher touches a sensitive spot in the hearers. Fr. David Murphy of the Washington Theological Consortium, himself an instructor in homiletics, has written at length on this in an article called "Inductive Preaching: Reaching People Where They Are" (*The Priest,* June 1978). When the preacher touches that sensitive spot in the congregation, they will know that they have been reached "where they live," where they have a stake, a vested interest. The word of God has not been adapted or manipulated to fit them; it has been applied to them at the point where they are open, a truly human point of vulnerability.

The preacher who fails to do this starts with a subject when he should be starting with an object. The preacher's real concern is with the day-to-day problems and thoughts of his people, shaped by media, culture, faith, school, etc. Nothing that he can say—however wise, clever, original, or world-shattering—matters much until he makes contact with the thinking people of his congregation. The preacher who helps people understand their own lives and see their way to faith is performing a real service. He need not solve their problems. He just must let them know he understands and that God understands too—at the same time calling them forward to deeper faith and conversion. He must reassure them of God's love and that his gracious mercy and power abound over our sins and weaknesses. He must affirm a presence of God that makes faith, hope and love possible when their bones feel weary and dry.

Caution!

I recall an experience in which I myself violated the above canons of congregational concern.

On the weekend following the end of the Vietnam War, I preached to a congregation which was heavily military and CIA/FBI. I was eager to share my happiness over the end of the war, but I had only helped out in this parish twice before, so I didn't know any of the people. In a sense, I was a Sunday intruder!

What I considered was a good sermon—carefully prepared and all—failed badly. I could feel the hostility in the congregation. People leaving the Church were mute, with a couple of exceptions. One person, a teenager, whose parents had lived under Stalinist persecutions, told me he would never go to Mass again. He could not understand why I would welcome an American pullout in Vietnam which left the Vietnamese people abandoned to Communism.

I am convinced, in retrospect, that I could have preached the same message differently had I done more congregational analysis. Obviously, some people would have reacted negatively no matter what I said, the Vietnam War being as polarizing as it was. But I could have reached more people. The congregation immediately felt defensive. It was my "peace" ideology against their different point of view. I should have spoken with one of the parish priests to get a deeper insight into the congregation. He might have helped me to shape my message differently.

Obviously the preacher will meet opposition no matter what he says or how he says it. American congregations are generally too complex to allow the preacher to reach everyone positively. Vast crowds followed Jesus. Some listened; others threw stones. However, I believe that the preacher's task is to try to reach as many people as possible and never to write off a congregation as hopeless. Some who at first respond negatively might discern on further reflection God's stirrings within them so that a conversion could take place.

It isn't easy to sense where the congregation is ideologically—even in a relatively established small parish. Radio, TV, newspapers, cultural and political prejudices and casual opinions are too deeply rooted in their lives. Add to this the fact that many people feel abandoned by God or that the Church doesn't understand or care for them. No wonder they keep asking, "Why, why, why?"

It's a herculean task to give a congregation a feeling and sense of God's care and the Church's pastoral solicitude in ten or so minutes on Sunday. The preacher has to take hold of real difficulties in the lives and thoughts of the people. As he tries to meet their needs, he cannot preach dogmatically about solutions. He tries to enter into a trusting relationship with his people and to think through their faith questions and hopes with them.

Woman at the Well: Relationship Begins

After all, isn't that what Jesus did with the woman at the well? He talked with her. He knew exactly what her life was like. He wasn't embarrassed about it. She simply was what she was. When Jesus focused on her five former husbands and the man she was now living with, the woman changed the subject. She flattered him, saying, "I see that you are a prophet. Our ancestors worshiped on this mountain."

Jesus could have given her dogma, or scolded her, or preached to her. Rather, he chose the positive way of winning her devotion, calling her to something deeper in her life—her need for love and faith. She ended up by shouting enthusiastically about what had happened to her: "Come and see someone who told me everything I ever did. Could this not be the Messiah?"

The preacher's invitation to the people, through his sermon, is to help the congregation meet Jesus or to set out, as did the disciples, to new places where Jesus is to be found. In this instance, Jesus took hold of a real problem of the Samaritan woman, stated it better than she, and proceeded to establish a relationship—frankly, fairly and helpfully. He made her think. She might have been embarrassed, but she followed him in the relationship. He was dealing with something vital to her. So, too, the preacher deals with something vital to his listeners. When they feel this, they will respond. Using good pedagogy, the preacher can help the listener raise questions himself. The listeners believe that they thought it all up for themselves; it has happened in their own minds. They may *think* it was a great sermon but they *know* they've met a great God!

A Pastoral Approach

Take prejudice, for example—a worthy subject for preaching. You take the congregation through some of the reasons why racial and ethnic prejudices exist. You let them know that you understand how prejudices exist. You let them know that you understand how prejudice can appear to be reasonable. You do not, however, *accuse* them of being prejudiced. You do not say that they have to change because Jesus showed no prejudice against the Samaritan woman. You take them through their feelings without judgment. As a preacher, you draw on your own experiences of prejudice: you understand their feelings because some of theirs are the same as yours. The wise preacher does not build his sermon on a dogmatic monologue telling people what to believe, with promises of divine retribution if they do not change, nor does he appeal immediately to the Church's authority. No, the preacher appeals to reason and feelings. He raises objections. Fears, clarifications, doubts, and guilt are mentioned up front and fairly dealt with. He articulates their feelings. The end of the sermon may sound like this:

The Church, reflecting on its own experience of Jesus and measuring its performance by his Gospel, has had to admit prejudice in some of its relationships with Jews, blacks, and Orientals. The Holy Spirit always purifies and changes our hearts. He leads us to new insights and teachings, and calls us away from prejudice. The documents of Vatican II, the public statements of Popes John XXIII and Paul VI, and John Paul I and II, lead us to new understanding of the unity of all peoples and their human rights. Jesus refused to accept the limitations and boundaries imposed on him by the prejudices of his culture. He was compassionate and understanding of women who, in his time, had no rights; he talked with and visited and ate with people who were outcasts in his society. He invites *us* to go beyond the bounds of prejudice and hatred toward those who are different from us. Now that we are baptized and enjoy a special relationship to the Father through Jesus, we are one in the Lord. "There is neither Greek nor Jew nor slave nor free man," St. Paul says. "We are all one in Christ."

This requires some knowledge of what people are thinking, how they are thinking, and why they are thinking as they do. For me as a preacher to engage you as a listener, I must communicate some sense that I *appreciate* why you think as you do, without passing judgment—at least not immediately. A persuasive preacher might express his own judgment to the people that some conversion is necessary to live the Gospel.

Social Gospel and Preaching

For example, I might say, "I know that some of you would not agree that political issues like boycotting lettuce are religious issues. I hope I understand why you don't agree. For one thing, I know that for years—especially during those years when many of us learned from the *Baltimore Catechism*—religion did not emphasize the relationship between a person's right to a just wage and the love of God. We didn't connect social issues to religion as strongly as we have done since the Second Vatican Council. There always were devout Catholics involved in social justice issues, but some of their ideas didn't filter down to us in our Catholic publications. So it isn't our fault that we find it hard to connect social struggle with religion. We've been conditioned to think that they are separate issues. Today we will examine together why so much Church teaching on social issues appears to have changed. We will look at some biblical texts which invite us to wrestle with the Church's belief that the love of God can be related to a lettuce boycott."

When done well, this kind of preaching possesses important qualities. It is not militant, pugnacious, or judgmental. Nor is it condescending or patronizing. It is irenic, kind, constructive, and reasonable. It appeals to personal experience. It lays no guilt at the door of the listener. It respects persons as they are, often through no fault of their own. We have had our fill of guilt trips laid on congregations by social activists, campaigns against sin and perdition by righteous crusaders, enemy attacks, and epithets hurled by those who disagree with authority. Sermons that try to meet the needs of the people and to fulfill the need to live a faith marked by love and compassion— these sermons will reach the people. Most people who believe in Jesus, who are at Mass on Sunday, want to love their enemies, and many struggle hard to do so. Most people want conversion of heart.

Sermons which try to answer people's questions, present alternatives for behavior without condemnation, and interpret their experiences in kind and understanding ways—such sermons are the preacher's task.

Dr. Harry Emerson Fosdick says, "There is nothing people are so interested in as themselves, their problems and the ways to solve them. No preaching that neglects this can raise a ripple on the congregation."

"Their problems and how to solve them"—this is one of the pastoral challenges which the pulpit confronts.

A Pastoral Choice

An example might help. I listened to a sermon after the Vatican's declaration on sexuality appeared about four years ago. The sermon was solemn. The preacher told the people, "especially you young people," that he was going to preach on a very important issue, namely sexuality, and added: "What I have to say you may not like to hear."

Clearly the priest had launched his sermon by drawing the battle lines. He was trying to be pastoral (showing concern about a real human problem) but his voice was angry, strident, and authoritarian. The gist of the whole sermon was that he knew that a lot of kids in the congregation were living together and did not accept the Church's teaching on sex, masturbation, abortion, etc. But with the Church's declaration on sexuality there were "no ifs, ands or buts about it." In effect he was saying: "We know what's sinful, and that's that!"

My critique of the sermon was that there was no invitation to anyone struggling and feeling pained and guilty to come and talk to him. "Come to me, all you who are burdened and heavy-laden. . . . " Had I been in the congregation, suffering from these problems, troubled by my own lack of sexual integrity, I could never have gone to that priest. The sermon lacked compassion, sympathy, and understanding. One may express the Church's teaching from the pulpit until doomsday. When pastoral concern and empathy are absent, there can be little hope of salvation. The people just turn the preacher off and say: "He doesn't care. If I go to him, I'll just get bawled out." Some just stay home. Often what this means pastorally is that the person in the pew is left totally alone: "Even God (i.e., the Church) has abandoned me. To whom shall I turn?"

The preacher, in this case, had a golden pastoral opportunity. He had made the decision to preach sex from the pulpit (a very difficult, but legitimate endeavor, by the way). Analysis of the congregation should have told him that there are very few normal people who don't struggle with some sexual problems. He could have alluded to the Vatican Declaration, since it had received so much press publicity. He could then have stressed the positive elements of the document, upholding a value. He could have said he understood that sexuality was very complex, and that he wasn't out to make judgments about anybody there, acknowledging that the culture had changed and people were confused and burdened. He could have included some statement that sexuality is a crucial dimension of our lives, since it determines how we relate with others. He could have mentioned how love combats loneliness and how the Holy Spirit is always working in us to help us achieve wholeness. Some stories of Jesus might have been helpful—how he dealt with people whom society condemned for their sexual sins. The sermons could have stated more pastoral concern with the people, urging them not to give up even if they found themselves in situations which they know to be contrary to the Church's traditionally understood teaching.

The preacher might have concluded with something like this: "We all need to talk things over with others, seek clarification, question how we are living and loving, renew our lives, and move in different directions. Now is a good time to do that. We ask God to look on our weakness with mercy and forgiveness and to lead us into new paths." The preacher might also have added an invitation to see him privately and talk about it, or to start a discussion group on sexuality.

Obviously the issue could be preached about in a number of pastoral ways. What is important is that the congregation feels that the preacher cares, that the Church cares, and that God cares and is near us in our human weakness.

Congregation Response and Critiquing

One interesting route a preacher might take would be to invite responses a week *previous* to his preaching. For example, the preacher could distribute texts for the approaching week to all of the people and tell them that he intends to preach on a certain subject—for example, forgiveness. He then asks the people to write down some of their thoughts on forgiveness, what it means to them, how they experience it in their lives, what they expect from the Church on forgiveness, their attitudes toward the sacrament of penance, confession, etc.

The response may not be startling, but this gives the people an opportunity to share their needs and expectations anonymously; it can also help the preacher to know: "Who, what and where are my people?"

Congregational critiquing of sermons can be helpful. The preacher asks various individuals in the congregation to critique the sermon and to attune themselves to what they hear others saying. An occasional request, with a critique form, given to members of the congregation will give the preacher an insight into how his sermons are being received. (See Appendix E.) While anonymous questionnaires can cause problems for this purpose, they are probably the best route to follow. I might add that candidates for ministry and priesthood are familiar with supervision and group-critiquing in their pastoral work, and many young priests are now asking for this to continue in their early years of priesthood.

Conclusion

Christianity is a religion of proclamation. Preaching is at the core of its meaning. No other world religion presumes to make preaching such an integral part of worship. Pulpit and altar stand side by side. Someone has said: "No other religion has ever made the regular and frequent assembly of the masses of men to hear religious instructions and exhortations so integral a part of divine worship."

Paul, a preacher without peer, knew his people—who, what, and where they were. "That is why I sent to find out about your faith when I could stand the suspense no longer," Paul writes. "But now, brothers, since Timothy has returned to us from you reporting the good news of your faith and love, and telling us that you constantly remember us and are as desirous to see us as we are to see you, we have been much consoled by your faith throughout our distress and trial" (1 Thes. 3:5-7).

God had one Son. He was a preacher. He knew the multitudes. He knew their innermost thoughts. He knew their joys, hopes, and pains, their thirst for God. He was in the crowds with them. He knew his people.

Can we, who speak his word, do less?

SPECIFIC POINTS AND EXERCISES FOR STUDY

From POINTS FOR PREPARATION AND DELIVERY (See *Introduction* I)

I. Make initial check:
   (a) World events, TV shows. Try to get a sense of what media or world events might shape the attitudes of your congregation during the week.
   (b) Congregation. What will it be like? Who will be there?
   (c) Liturgical Time and Event (Advent, Lent, Pentecost, Ordinary Time). How can this shape my message?
   (d) Jottings. Jot down ideas from texts, world events, parish happenings during the week—or anticipated events. Jot down thoughts, feelings, hints, reflections which come to mind during the week.

II. Take one or two pastoral concerns in the parish and outline several possible ways of integrating it within a sermon.

III. Jot down eight to ten words which best define or characterize your congregation—for example, mixed age groups, blue collar workers, university, etc. Think of the sermons you have given which have been well received and write down the reasons.

From EXERCISES AND REFLECTIONS TO ENHANCE PREACHING (See *Introduction* II)

I. Try full-length mirror practice. Get access to a full-length mirror (every seminary should have a sound-proof room with a full-length mirror), stand in front of it, talk, practice the homily, make faces, gesture freely and extravagantly. This exercise is fun and is given to help the speaker get accustomed to feeling comfortable with his body. Overexaggerate bodily movements, gestures, etc., in order to arrive at a happy medium with which you are comfortable and which is not contrived or artificial.

II. Monitor TV. Pick out two or three television personalities and keep a log on how they speak, words they use, images they form, etc. Observe how they relate to other people on the show. Media people are pros. We can learn from them. TV commercials hit us with action, imagery, repetition, value, all in one minute.

5.
From Pulpit to Pew: Communicating the Message

If ya gonna preach . . .
        Read yourself full
        Think yourself clear
        Pray yourself hot
            and then
        Let yourself go!

                                A Black Preacher

"Faith, then, comes through hearing, and what is heard is the word of Christ. I ask you, have they not heard?

                                Rom. 10:17-18

"I never hear a word Father says. He keeps his head down and mumbles. Why does he bother to preach? I don't even try to listen anymore. It's too much work."

A devout Catholic woman said this to me. She's no exception. Sunday after Sunday, congregations struggle to hear the words of the preacher. Once upon a time, people in the pews would complain that they couldn't hear the priest. The advent of microphones should have solved that problem. It hasn't. Microphones merely amplify the mumbling. Pew sitters still complain.

Way back with Aristotle, people understood the crucial elements for good communication: (1) speaker, (2) speech, (3) audience. Whether delivered from pulpit or podium, desk or deck, classroom or coliseum, attention to all three was a must. Sadly, the audience has too long been neglected.

Communication in the Mass Media

Much is being said about communication today. Daily, Americans listen to masters of the art. ABC, NBC, CBS and PBS bring clear, concise, styled language into our living rooms. Short comments on the news from Eric Severeid, Rod MacLeish, Howard K. Smith, Harry Reasoner and John Chancellor are models of syntax, imagery, style and precision. (See Appendix G for a model for short, daily homilies. It is a commentary by Rod MacLeish on Pope John Paul's visit to Poland.) TV also bombards us with junk fare. But the junk is well presented—often convincingly—even though the commentators are reading from a teleprompter or "idiot" cards. Specials, documentaries and drama impress on us the genius of mass media experts. Theirs is a secular ministry of verbal communication, but preachers would do well to imitate their expertise. The object is to get their message across in the most attractive and persuasive way possible. Communication involves both message and mood. It entails not only correct and distinct pronunciation of words in a voice that can be adequately heard, but also encompasses the transfer of emotional color and emphasis from one person to another. When either mood or meaning suffers, communication fails.

Religious Communication

Sacred communication is an attempt to interpret God's gestures to us. The preacher communicates from the pulpit and altar to help people meet Jesus in a saving way. Preaching is saying something about Jesus and ourselves. It is to proclaim what God the Father has done and said through Jesus about God's action in our lives. Preaching is done to give, restore and renew life in the hearer. To do that, we use words, symbols, gestures, signs and silence. As soon as the preacher steps in front of the people, they expect him to say something about God's saving deeds. Because communication is an act and a process, it does not happen just up there in your brain. It moves out of the brain and becomes part of all who hear. The sermon will be received as either negative or positive, according to the ability of your listener to translate your words into images shaped out of his or her needs.

Ministry (not just preaching) is synonomous with communication. Religious ministry's purpose is to help the receiver of the ministry feel that God is near—that he cares, that there is some union or covenant, or communion, with God. The word communication has many cousins: "communion," "community," "communize."

A religious communicator helps his listener to feel at one with God, himself, and others. He brings them into union with God through words, images and moods, just as consecrated bread comes into people's lives as Communion with Jesus. A preacher who mumbles, cannot be heard, is inarticulate, unclear and incoherent, cannot expect to be "at one" with his listeners. Neither can he hope to help the congregation be at one with God. Congregations simply turn off the preacher as they would turn off the TV set or radio when there is no kinship of word or mood.

Much in our society focuses attention on the art of communication. There are increasing demands for the preaching person to take more seriously his role as communicator. Liturgy's revival, Eastern prayer, yoga, and body cults make the congregation more attentive to "body language"—what a preacher is saying, symbolically, by his gestures, postures, eye contact (or lack of it). Where is he looking? "Why is he looking down at the pulpit during the entire sermon when I'm out here? He's speaking about the joy of Jesus but he looks like a sad sack. He's talking about being free in the Lord, but he's as tense as piano wire. Why does he keep rubbing his hands together as if they were sticks being frictioned for fire?"

Like it or not, body communication helps or hinders the message. President Woodrow Wilson put it in a nutshell. Reflecting on his teaching years at Princeton he said: "My strongest impression is that of the infinite capacity of the human mind to resist information."

Pastoral Ministry as Communication

All pastoral ministry is basically communication. It is an attempt to reveal the Christian faith and its freeing grace. The prime goal of the healing and helping profession is to enable people to communicate more freely with God and one another—to be "at one" with God, at one with oneself, at one with others, to share joys, griefs, faith, doubts, so as to feel part of, and a recipient of, God's saving acts within the community of believers.

A priest who shares his own faith with his congregation does more than tell what he believes; he encourages others to respond by sharing *their* faith. He taps the faith already in their hearts. He helps them to attain harmony with the Spirit already there. He attunes them to listen to the God praying within them.

A family counselor enables members of a troubled family to communicate with one another so that barriers are broken down. A speech therapist does more than correct stuttering or lisping; he puts new content into a person's self-image and thus opens new ways of relating to others. A preacher who communicates how he senses God's love in everyday life may free others to say how they find God there, too.

By virtue of ministry, then, the ministerial person is, by vocation, a communicator. Ministry *is* communication and communication *is* ministry. Jesus is God the Father's communication.

Take a look at your life as a ministerial person and you will see that communication is not just a pulpit event.

You awaken, turn on the radio, and hear the news of the day. *Good Morning, America* and the *Today Show* immediately plunge you into human events—tragedies, wars, fires, famines, floods, earthquakes, snowstorms, kidnapings, riots around the world. People tell their stories—how they fought cancer with hope, how they stopped smoking, why jogging is like a religious experience, how one person began a worldwide movement to help children who have cerebral palsy. Someone tells us how to cook a gourmet meal with vegetables only, or how personal faith kept hope alive after the loss of a child who died of leukemia.

At breakfast, if you live with other ministerial people, you might talk about plans for the day. "I'm going to spend the day in the hospital participating in a workshop on new approaches to ministering to the terminally ill," or "I'm meeting with the neighborhood ministerial association to explore ways to reach city officials about garbage not being collected in our poor, blighted areas."

You might then look at the newspaper. At some point in the day, you read a book (communication through the printed word), listen to a cassette on preaching to children (communication through the spoken word at long range), then write a rough draft of your upcoming sermon (communication through literary expression for anticipated communication).

The phone rings. On the other end you hear the voice of a desperate woman whose marriage is on the rocks. The doorbell sounds. A relatively calm young man asks to speak to you. During the conversation you size him up by his body language. He is emotionally distraught, tense, and angry. He masks his feelings by trying to be cool. By simply listening and watching, except to nod occasionally or to say "I understand," you communicate acceptance and caring. You establish some "union" or "communion" with him. Your communication of understanding and caring frees him to speak to you truthfully so that you can help him.

And so it is. The day goes on: meetings, talks, homilies, a chat on the street with a parishioner who introduces you to a stranger. Some routine calls. That evening you anoint a dying person. The sacraments are a special kind of communication, through sign and symbol, of the presence of Christ.

Reflecting that night, you realize: "My whole ministry is communication." And then you wonder "What will I preach about this Sunday?" as you nod off to sleep to communicate in your dreams.

Communication Theory:
Source, Encoding, Signal, Decoding, Congregation

Communication theories abound. The preacher's ministry is helped if he understands at least one of them. The Shannon-Weaver model has five elements to it. (1) The *source:* that from which (or whom) the message comes—in other words, the preacher. He might decide to use slides, films, tapes, or his own words, but they are all still part of the source. Then there is (2) *encoding:* putting the idea into words. Obviously the words make the difference between darkness and light. What words will say best what I want my congregation to hear? It is at this point that the preacher decides whether he will use simple language, images, stories, technical language, theological or psychological jargon. He may decide to be mainly non-verbal: show a picture, flourish a banner, or even use pantomime.

Now the preacher moves into (3) the *signal:* that is, the carrier of the message. First and obvious are the body parts which God gave us: our lips, tongue, larynx, resonating chambers, etc., which generate the sound. The better tuned up and synchronized these are, the clearer the message. Electrical equipment such as microphones and amplifiers are all part of this.

Through all of this there is the work of (4) *decoding the message.* This is crucial. The audience or congregation has to do this. This is the point at which the listener makes contact with the source, the preacher. Decoding ministerial communication is critical.

For example, you might decide to encode your sermon in "rock" idiom for teenagers, using their language, music, banners or multimedia. That's fine for youngsters. But what about older members of the congregation? You may be talking to the wall. The elders have no way to decode this. The words and images are too alien to their understanding of the Gospel. You might subvert your message entirely and reach only a few. A constant challenge in preaching is to encode a message so that the *majority* of people can decode its meaning.

Last is the destination, or (5) *congregation.* Your destination as ministerial communicator may range from the lone person sitting across from you in the parlor to the throngs in the pews. To get the message across, the speaker has to know his destination. An exchange of roles occurs at this point. The preacher must put himself into his hearers' shoes. The congregation has to say, on the other hand, "What would I be saying if I were in his place? What does he mean by that word? Does it mean to him what it means to me? What do 'eschatological,' 'consubstantiation,' and 'external principle' mean?"

A recent example comes to mind. Prior to the televised funeral of Pope Paul VI, one channel interviewed a bishop who said that Pope Paul's greatest contribution was his respect for "natural life." The bishop didn't say what he meant by "natural life." A Protestant person who was watching TV with me asked: "What does he mean by 'natural life'? Protection of nature, like ecology? Or is he referring to abortion?" I had to answer, "I don't know."

I *suspected,* but I didn't know. In this case, since this bishop wanted to say something specific about Pope Paul's greatest contribution, he should have communicated more clearly and said exactly what he meant. It was a good case of the source not sizing up the destination. "Natural life" can mean anything from amoeba to zebra, Adam to Zoraster.

SMCR Model

David K. Berlo's SMCR Model has four basic concepts of communication: (1) Source (2) Message (3) Channel and (4) Receiver. Like other models, it combines some of all. For Berlo, the preacher, or *source,* cannot be discussed apart from his communication skills, attitudes, knowledge and the social-culture system in which he was raised.

The *message* has elements, structure, content, treatment and code. Translated, that means words, sentences, ideas, pictures, music, banners, etc. The way the preacher brings all of these together and organizes the inter-relationship between words and music, banners and visual aids relates to the structure of the elements.

The preacher's central idea determines its content. How does he bring all the elements together to get the listeners to focus on his core message—what he wants them to take from the pew into their homes?

Treatment is the way in which the preacher weaves the web of decisions that determines his content, structure, delivery and personal style. The encoding process in the sermon is the search for persuasive, precise language, illustrations, symbols and images to express the central idea.

The *channel* of his sermon is simply the "what" he will use to get the message to its destination. Phone? Letter? Senses? Taste? Smell? Body contact? Microphone? Tape recorder? This is the dangerous area. Gimmickry is likely to rear its ugly head at this point. It is the "make or break" point. It is at this juncture that the congregation puts up the most resistance and feels manipulated. It's at this moment that the congregation sizes up the preacher as real or phony.

Proclamation as Receivership

Berlo's theory focuses last on the *receiver*. This is the congregation. It is in the area of receivership that an interacting occurs. The receiver also has to have listening skills, attitudes, and knowledge. Like the source, the congregation lives in a social and cultural system. Because communication is an interaction process (to become "in-union" with someone else) there is always interaction going on between listener and source. There is constant interplay. The congregation is thinking thoughts—some good, some bad—about the preacher: "Gee, he's good," or, "I should have stayed in bed!" Rustling in the pews, fidgeting with purses, mulling over the missalettes, wondering who that attractive couple is—these occur here.

The preacher enters into a reverse role. He also becomes a receiver as he observes the pew-receivers. Their facial expressions tell him something; their grimaces, nods, twitching, attention, silence and fidgeting are cueing the preacher in on their mood: "I'm with you, baby," or, "Man, sit down!" So the primary receiver (the congregation) is always bringing to the process of communication its own messages, attitudes, openness, withdrawal, antagonisms, boredom—its own knowledge of Scripture, the world, its own pre-conceptions, social attitudes, prejudices, biases, preferences. In a pluralistic congregation, source and receiver may have basic, differing identifications.

This is borne out by a recent conversation with a friend who lives in a suburban parish of a large city noted for its many universities. The educational level of the parish is high. Almost all residents are college graduates; many are professionals: doctors, lawyers, high-level government employees. Many priests from Africa and Asia assist in this parish on Sundays.

My friend complains that it is difficult to understand the English of the assisting priests. For one thing, they use microphones badly, amplifying their halting English. My friend's further criticism is that these preachers do not understand the culture in which they are living—our culture. They impose their own categories on the congregation. The people feel patronized.

One preacher always speaks as if he is teaching catechism to African children living in remote villages. He cannot identify culturally with his congregation in the United States. A basic ingredient of communication falls by the wayside: interaction. The source lives in a vastly different world than the receiver. Add to this all the other ingredients that are lacking—language, structure, treatment, etc.— and the result is that very little proclamation is taking place.

While this is a whole new issue which requires treatment in another forum, suffice to say that, from the point of view of preaching, it poses a serious pastoral problem.

Many courses in homiletics are entitled along the lines of "Preaching: Verbal Communication" or "The Art of Sacred Communication." This is good, for it announces preaching as communication, as art.

One layman who teaches communication as a dramatic art form describes good preaching in five steps. He calls them the "psychologically motivated sequence." It is the unfolding of an idea. This theory is helpful because of its simplicity.

"Ho-Hum" Crashers; Attention

There are five steps. The first is (1) *attention.* This is what "grabs" people. It can be an incident, narrative, image or story. Someone else has called it a "ho-hum" crasher. This appeals to the power of image and imagination in our lives. Our imagination never goes to sleep. Even when the congregation is getting in a catnap during the sermon, imagination is working furiously: daydreams, fantasies, building castles in the sky. The story or incident is an attempt to crash through all the "ho-hums" in the congregation, to stir their immediate interests, clear out the cobwebs, dissipate the area between wakefulness and sleep. The opener in a sermon has to cause the listener to say: "Hmm, I think I'll listen."

Bible characters, an incident from one's life, a dramatic occurrence during the week, a statement of self-interest to the congregation—any of these could be used as attention-getters. The stronger and more direct—the simpler the attention-getter—the better. "Ho-hum" crashers should revolve around people, places, happenings, or conversations between characters in Scripture. People are moved by hearing what events and happenings shape the lives of others. People identify strongly with other people, places, and events. That is what feeds us in our lives; it is what feeds our faith. In a negative way, it's what feeds gossip columnists. In a positive way, it's what attracts people to Abigail Van Buren ("Dear Abby") and Ann Landers. Knowing the Jesus event and the people in his life feeds our faith. Attention-getters are about concrete human events and lives. This is the power of the parable, the myth, the story, the fairy tale. They are concrete; they appeal to our imagination. Logical or abstract syllogisms in preaching may feed one's intellect but rarely nourish one's heart.

Need

Next in line to attention is (2) *need*. When the preacher shares an experience that makes the congregation want to hear more, it is because the listener feels that what he hears could make a difference in his or her life. Thus is a need fulfilled. When the preacher touches deeply where the congregation hurts, fears, despairs or hopes, he has touched "need."

For example, the preacher may describe an experience of sin that is universal: the sin of greed. This is rooted in human nature. Most people will listen. Another universal need is to experience freedom from fear. How does the preacher touch the need of the congregation—rich or poor, young or old, lettered or unlettered—to feel loved, forgiven, to feel part of something bigger than oneself?

This is the problem of loneliness versus communal sharing. When the preacher is talking about something in life that affects everyone deeply, people will sit on the edges of their seats and all ears will perk. Abortion, birth control, infallibility, obedience to authority—all these topics have their place in pastoral preaching. However, I'd venture to say that for *most* people in the pews, these issues are not crucial to their daily lives, and thus they create little or no need to listen.

Satisfaction

Next in the motivation sequence is (3) *satisfaction.* Once you establish a need in someone, you then try to satisfy it. Pills, meditation cults, drugs, alcohol—these fulfill some deep need in their users: to escape from or to dull pain, to experience a sense of otherness or to hide from fear. In some way these crutches are salvific and freeing. Only when the congregation experiences a *need* to be saved can the preacher speak effectively of a Savior.

Visualization

Satisfaction relates closely to (4) visualization and image. In the Christian way of things, God becomes visible in Jesus. Jesus shows us the way to salvation by telling stories and parables. The Gospel writers did the same. They create images in my mind. If I were to ask you to accept a way of life in my preaching and to take some action to live that life, then I would want you to visualize what will happen if you don't do this. When the listener in the pew cannot visualize "what would happen if," then it is likely that he will continue doing or living exactly as he is now. Living differently (conversion) needs to be considered better or more fulfilling than living the way one is now. It is the power of the word, the imagination, that joins the Holy Spirit in moving the congregation.

Action

Finally, the preacher moves toward (5) *action.* This is simply encouragement: to speak, pray, act, give, and live in the new directions brought about by the interior movement toward conversion which the sermon has prompted. This encouragement can be a simple pastoral urging to try to find a new direction, to work during the week to see things differently and to try to experience the difference in your life.

For example, there are many stories in Scripture where Jesus speaks to outsiders. Among them are the Canaanite and Samaritan women. He did so usually at the risk of scandalizing the onlookers.

These people didn't fit into the category of the "saved" or "worthy." In the context of a sermon, some gentle pastoral encouragement to work toward combating prejudice in the language we use with each other, or toward accepting ethnic or racial groups, is a simple step toward conversion. To pray for a melting away of prejudice or hatred or the habit of stereotyping people is an action step. To correct our children who use words such as "spic," "nigger," "ginzo," or "polack" is a move toward conversion of heart, toward building up a community of love and care. The language we use begins to make a difference in the way we see people and relate to them. This conversion can be a grace that leads to more sensitive and caring relationships, toward understanding Jesus' teaching "to love one another."

I am always impressed with the ways in which businesses train employees on various levels to be more effective communicators. Preaching courses could use their methods without in any way violating the integrity of sacred elocution. These courses involve appealing presentation, the reaction of the audience to the message, ways and means by which people are moved to listen so that a product can be sold. Congregations have every right to expect that those who preach to them will value communication as an art, even more than those who work to sell commercial products.

Common Speech Faults

Finally, a few points about common speech faults. The paperback *A Handbook for Lectors* by William Carr (Paulist Press) articulates common problems of communication—problems which stand in the way of distinctness. Some are obvious: too much voice, too little voice, talking too rapidly, dropping the ends of sentences and words, ellision of words, contraction, drawling, the insertion of "ah, ah, ah," poor enunciation and adding syllables or letters. Poor vocalization qualities (strident, flat, weak voices), inertia, bad pitch, bad emphasis, lulling speech, non-modulated words, bad pause habits, no change of rate, jerkiness, lack of feeling—all of these are the common speech faults on which our message travels to the people.

They are common faults. Asking someone to criticize your speech or listening to yourself on a tape-recorder can be helpful. The first step in improving speech for better communication, of course, is the desire to improve it—and then to practice.

Without this desire, the preacher stands in danger of speaking to deaf ears.

Conclusion

It is a happy day when congregations throughout the country grow ever more critical of poor sermons. Expectations are rising. Seminaries, in taking preaching more seriously, are offering a wider range of courses in homiletics. It's a pity, though, that preaching is still not yet on a par with academic courses such as dogma or Scripture. What we need are more preaching courses—from basic speech and communication methods, to preaching content. Preaching is often a course the seminarian "squeezes" into his curriculum. One course suffices before ordination. Why not a preaching course each year of seminary education, beginning with basic communication and writing skills to proclamation? Why not allocate more academic funds for larger homiletics faculties? As priests get busier and busier, there may be a tendency for the sermon to get short shrift. "I don't have time to prepare" is still a common complaint. The preacher is asked to spend his days and weeks in committee meetings, group discussions, and new forms of pastoral outreach on a scale never before so broad. His seminary curriculum prepares him intellectually with the best in theological background. Why not preaching and writing? Seminaries must strive for ways to teach skills of translating the content into words and images which will move congregations to faith. Without such an effort, noble movements such as evangelization and catechesis are in peril, and a generation hence may spell the end of religious literacy among a broad spectrum of American Catholics.

Those who are serious about buttressing the art of preaching can take comfort in words of an interested critic of the preaching scene: "Not all are ordained to teach. But all are ordained to preach."

In short, those commissioned to preach are commissioned to communicate.

SPECIFIC POINTS AND EXERCISES FOR STUDY

From POINTS FOR PREPARATION AND DELIVERY (See *Introduction* I)

I. Structure the Sermon.
   (a) Outline and block out. Decide on the introduction. Relate this to the curiosity of the listeners, catching and holding interest.
   (b) Decide on key words to be repeated throughout the sermon to keep the congregation focused on the theme (observe TV ads: they repeat the product name or catchy phrases for you to remember).
   (c) Develop central theme with clear examples: Point one, e.g., point two, e.g., point three, e.g.
   (d) Amplify theme with these examples.
   (e) Use direct, clear, simple language. Keep it concrete. Use image words.
   (f) Cut out theological or philosophical jargon.
   (g) For the conclusion, return to the introduction. Summarize and exhort.

II. Write/Rewrite.
   (a) Develop the points in the section above. Move from outline to prose development. Keep asking: Could I say this more simply? With more imagery? Review, rewrite, cut. Cut—even if it means parting with a gem. Ask: Does this sentence or word hinder or help my sermon? Remember: attention not won in the first couple of minutes is never won at all.
   (b) Get rid of the " if's," "let us," "shoulds" and "oughts."

III. Read Aloud.
   (a) Practice in front of a mirror. If possible, tape or video-tape. Practice over the public address system. Be conscious of your voice.
   (b) Underline words you want to emphasize. Keep refining the sermon as you listen to yourself. Get a feel of delivery and a sense of gestures—when they should occur.

(c) Keep asking: Will the congregation know what I mean when I use this or that word? Does it deal with real life? Or is it esoteric? Unrelated? Is it about their life or *speculation* about life? Remember: theology often speculates. The Bible deals with concrete circumstances of human life and the ways in which God breaks in.

IV. Critique

Arrange for a variety of people—young, elderly, married, single, middle-aged, from various education levels—to give you feedback on your sermons. Does your preaching reach them? Do you get the point across? What concrete suggestions can they make to improve your preaching as a pastoral event?

From EXERCISES AND REFLECTIONS TO ENHANCE PREACHING (See *Introduction* II)

I. Monitor TV. Pick out two or three television personalities and keep a log on how they speak, words they use, images they form, etc. Observe how they relate to other people on the show. Media people are pros. We can learn from them. TV commercials hit us with action, imagery, repetition, value, all in one minute.

6.
Images in Preaching:
A Theatre in Your Head

"In the image of God he created him."

Gen. 1:27

"When I was a kid, I always drew pictures, made images. That's how the mind works—in pictures. It has always been magical to me that a stream of thought is an evolution of pictures, like a theatre in your head."

James Pelletier
Artist

"Like a theatre in your head."

The sacred writer projects pictures into our minds. He has a deep feeling for words which reach into our hearts. These words, clear and simple, speak of vitality and vividness. They open doors to Jesus. Images let us see him. "In him we see our God made visible and so are caught up in love of the God we cannot see," the Christmas Preface tells us.

Our minds are like screens on which the God-event flashes. "Let the waters teem with an abundance of living creatures and all kinds of winged birds."

"He will wipe away every tear," the Book of Revelation promises.

And so it is. From Genesis to Revelation, God shapes his image in our hearts through pictures drawn by words.

When sin was born, the promises of its wages were cast in a scene of human drudgery: "By the sweat of your face shall you get bread to eat, until you return to the ground from which you were taken. For you are dirt, and to dirt you shall return."

Choice of Words: Beware of Abstract Language

Abstract words were not part of God's vocabulary. To him belong images of nature, strong emotions and feelings. Ezekiel "eats the word of the Lord." God purifies Isaiah's lips with a burning coal. The language of Jesus prefers action words, drama and movement ("Lukewarm? I will vomit you out of my mouth!") and vivid images of the body ("My bones cry out to you, O Lord").

The homilist's task is to move his listeners' hearts, just as the sacred writer did. He must flash figures into the minds of the congregation so that God's footsteps may be seen in our everyday land.

The choice of words for a homilist is, of course, important. The preaching person makes that choice. To choose abstract, philosophical or theological words with no corresponding image, or to choose words with corresponding pictures—that is the choice he must make.

Both students of homiletics and priests were, for a long time, notorious for framing their messages in heavy, abstract or theological jargon. For many years, until within the last decade or so, they spent several years in studies in which little or few connections were made between theology and life. Pre-ordination fare was filled with technical and Latinized terminology. Much of it, then, went untranslated into lived experience. Ontic, existential, architectonic, ecclesiological, hermeneutical, essence, ontological, efficacy, intrinsic, valid, definitively, mystical, omniscient, eternal, eschatological, transubstantiation, consubstantiation, indefectibility, redemptive—these are all uncommon words in life, but common in the pulpit. Fortunately, seminary education continues to change in the direction of theological-pastoral integration—a good sign, indeed!

I once heard a sermon delivered to many hundreds of people in a large basilica on the First Sunday of Advent. The opening words went something like this: "Today begins the holy season in which the pre-existent Logos is awaited so that he may usher in the eschatological promise of everlasting life."

I thought: "How exciting! I can't wait!"

Such a tangle of words are often simply a cover-up for the preacher's inability to express his faith in real words that will move another to faith. This kind of pretentious, esoteric preaching turns off even the most intelligent listeners. They are bored.

Recently I gave a talk to a group of novices. I wanted to say that God's word is always "efficacious." I said it purposely. "I don't like using that word," I told them, "but it expresses what I want to say. Does anyone know what it means?"

Silence. Then one man said, laughingly. "Yes, it means baloney." Laughter.

Getting back to business I said to him: "If I tell you that I will meet you promptly at eight o'clock tomorrow morning to jog, and you can be sure my word is efficacious, what do I mean?"

"That you can be trusted to be there," he responded.

"Fine," I said. "Now you know what 'efficacious' means."

It was a long way around to get to the meaning of a word. The point is that few people, even educated ones, are at home with philosophical and theological language because it has not been part of their day-to-day language. It is a little like seeing a menu of foreign foods; someone has to be there to translate the chef's offerings into images I can taste from my experience of other foods before I can begin to make a choice for dinner.

When students cast sermons into theological jargon, I ask them to take the same sermon and rewrite it, using image words as substitutes for every abstract term. I would underline for them all the words which called for substitute images. It was their task to find the right words. Occasionally, I would rewrite whole paragraphs for them to show them options for saying the same thing in simpler, clearer, more concrete Anglo-Saxon English.

Simplicity and Image

This exercise is difficult for seminarians and priests. In some ways it is difficult for Americans in general who come through a school system in which writing, language, and grammar have become stepchildren of the classroom.

Some schools don't teach writing anymore. GRE and college boards attest to growing literary and grammatical illiteracy. The potential preacher has two strikes against him if he has neither learned to write nor been trained to see and use the power of words.

Most of us, over the past decade or so, have been bombarded by professional administrative jargon. It has come out of the Pentagon, therapy groups, the White House, congressional hearings and technical journals. The language appears to obfuscate rather than clarify. Good speaking, like good writing, loves clear, accurate and vivid words.

Pope John Paul I: A Model

Shortly after the election of Albino Luciani as Pope John Paul I, the *Wall Street Journal* hailed him for his clear, unpretentious language. More than his smile, it thought that John Paul's unique gift among world leaders was his ability "to sense and use the power of language in moving people's hearts."

What the *Wall Street Journal* said about the Pope fits the preacher, too. Most ideas, the writer noted, come to life as language. The problem is "the sluggish ways in which public persons express themselves." John Paul's election to the papacy "promoted him to a brotherhood of world leadership joined by a common bond of dull articulation." What set him apart, in such a short time, was Luciani's first public statements, "cast in vivid, coherent (much needed) directness not heard in the world for some time," the article concluded.

The preacher does well when he simply imitates the style of the Bible writer. That style is concrete, dynamic, and utilizes simple words to describe the flow of life. To study the Bible for style alone will aid the preaching person.

An abstract style, for example, would note: "Life is fleeting and transitory and eventually we are assumed into the great beyond and enter eternal life."

But, to say that concretely, might sound like this: "Life moves fast. Things come and go. Before we know it, death meets us and takes us by the hand. It leads us into new life."

Bethlehem, Bethany, Nazareth, and the Sea of Galilee are more concrete, are they not, than the "places and towns where Jesus walked"?

The teacher asks: When is the last time you got excited by a syllogism? When did a virtual distinction or a canonical principle lead you to an image of faith that God is near or move you toward conversion of life?

Church people are not the only ones who get caught up in their esoteric language however. Doctors do this too! Professional medical language describes illness to a patient who has no inkling of what the jargon means. I have often thought it to be a gigantic conspiracy to keep the patient ignorant, as if he had no right to know clearly the condition of his own body.

Private language sounds learned—as if the medical school or seminary had done its work, but in reality it usually is only pompous and patronizing. A good preacher will make it a rule never to use an abstract term if a concrete one will serve, and likewise never to use a polysyllabic word if a single syllable word can be found.

Remember! God spoke simply. He cast sublime mysteries of life and death and love and hope into words we can still understand. He spoke to shepherds, fishermen, prostitutes, wine-dressers and smelly nomads. Each word in the Bible unfolds the mystery of God to man. Each word is God's word and each word comes from life's experiences. Tell the congregation that Jesus gave us bread rather than "he indulged in an act of generosity." With no problem, the intellect will supply the conclusion through the image.

The preacher is in the pulpit to move people to deeper faith and hope, not to impress them with erudition. "There are no great preachers," someone said. "There is only a great Gospel that bids us to proclaim it." Good Anglo-Saxon English does not require a stiff, stilted or abstract cast. It demands simple, familiar, concrete words. Good movies, poets, novelists, and TV commentators hold the attention of millions of people because they appeal to image. The writers have taken time to shape their words. There is a naturalness about the familiar words in our language in which thought can shape itself in the mind. Eric Severeid's two-minute commentaries were master-pieces of erudition framed in simple, concrete language.

Anglo-Saxon Word Power

Latin and Greek, so familiar to priests of yesterday's seminary, still mold pulpit language rather than the more homely, common Anglo-Saxon words. So much of our literature has had a heritage from the imitation of Latin and French models instead of a native English product. Latin may add to the exactness of language, help us with the root meanings of words and be a valuable addition to our stock of words, but it can never be a substitute for our own words. The Bible, especially the King James version, has the largest propor-tion of Anglo-Saxon words of any book in our literature. Yet it speaks with an emotional power and with a majesty of music and form no other book can equal. The Bible deals with the most intense and universal of human feelings and emotions; it speaks directly to the heart; it has overturned people's lives in dramatic ways. It de-scribes a life of action, of energy and enthusiasm, of conflict and peace. It does not concern itself with scientific or philosophical sub-tleties, though its philosophy of human life is profound. Anglo-Saxon words give us a literature of power. A good rule of thumb for the preacher who writes out his sermons is to use always the simplest im-age words that accurately convey the thought.

Words of Power and Action

Ezekiel dramatizes the power of image to depict the action of the Holy Spirit—the vague Person of the Trinity we have such diffi-culty capturing in words. Ezekiel sets the scene: a desert where a bat-tle once raged. The dead are there. Their remains are bleached bones. Try to imagine something more dead than bleached bones upon des-ert sands. God asks Ezekiel: "Son of man, can these bones live? Eze-kiel answers: "O Lord God, you alone know that." And God breathed his spirit across those dry bones and living men stood to their feet and marched across the desert, like a mighty army. God did this for Ezekiel's nation. The Spirit of God gives vitality, power, life and hope. But we want to be able to imagine that possibility. Someone once said: "Language in the pulpit is like an arrow. It must be clean and hit the target directly." St. Augustine asks: "What is the value to me of a gold key if it does not open the door I wish, or what is the harm of a wooden one if it does?" A congregation which must sit and wrestle with vagueness spends its time and energy trying to open the door.

Concreteness

I like the example of one writer who says in a homiletics journal: "You have a pork chop. Imagine a little boy. He smells it; he asks what's wrong with it." His father, obviously a learned man, says: "It is undergoing a process of decomposition in the formation of a new chemical compound." The boy probably wouldn't understand. How about saying: "It's rotten"? The boy would then immediately hold his nose. *Action follows image!* "Rotten" is a good Anglo-Saxon word and we don't have to go running to Webster to find its meaning. When Lazarus, dead for three days in a tomb, emerged, he "stank." That's better than "an odor was emitted from him," or "He smelled." Both "rotten" and "stink" are good Anglo-Saxon words, our own words.

Back to Augustine: a preacher who fails to use language which the people can understand defeats the purpose of preaching, which is to communicate the word of God. Use simple words. "Unless you're a genius," Augustine continues, "nothing but the habitual use of the smaller and better known words will assure you a simple style." High falutin, several-syllable words or lofty florid phrases may make you feel set apart from the crowd and might even please some, but they will not profit them. The person in the pew must follow your words, not work hard to keep figuring out what they mean. Henri Nouwen understands that a good preacher will evoke the feeling of "yes" when he touches the experience of the listener. "Yes, that's right, go on, tell me more. You're right. You understand me." The contrary is the congregation which has to keep saying: "What? What do you mean? What does that mean?"

One student of mine objected that simple, concrete words might lead the preacher into crudity and actually limit his choice of words.

It is true that crude words are often simple and vivid—those "four letter words" that evoke such clear images. However, crudity and simplicity are not synonomous. The use of imagination is not without danger; divorced from reality it can run wild. Unrestrained imagination often desecrates truth and detracts from beauty. Integrity and relationship to the people's lives must be the source of the imagination's discipline. When image becomes the servant of truth, it is a great asset, with a power to make truth come alive. I feel that the use of crude image-words and even acceptable crude parlance among people of faith are out of place in the pulpit. Only a very clever and recognizably holy person can get away with the use of crudity in the pulpit to illustrate a point. It is best to stay away from it. Vividness need not be crude and tasteless.

Biblical Image

Psalm 104 is one of the finest examples of biblical imagery I know. It is a hymn to God as Creator. From beginning to end, the writer triggers our imagination:

O Lord, my God, you are great indeed.
You are clothed with majesty and glory, robed in light as with
    a cloak.
You have spread the heavens like a tent cloth, you have built
    your palace upon the waters.

You make the clouds your chariot,
    you travel on the wings of the wind.
You make the winds your messengers,
    and flaming fire your ministers.

With the ocean as a garment,
    you covered it, above the mountains the waters stood.

At your rebuke, they fled,
    at the sound of your thunder they took to flight;
As the mountains rose, they went down the valleys
    to the place you had fixed for them.

You raise grass for the cattle,
   and vegetaion for men's use,
Producing bread from the earth
   and wine to gladden men's hearts.

To be steeped in the biblical world of image and language is the key to moving people's hearts. A preacher's growth is tied to reading and reflecting on the Scriptures, not only as a source of faith, but as a study of the language which helps him to experience how God speaks to us. The psalmist, the prophets, Jesus, Peter and Paul—all were steeped in image. The psalmist speaks about the power of God: "He scatters the hoarfrost like ashes." Jesus talks about the hypocrites: "You brood of vipers," about the fearful: "He has kept my eyes from tears, my feet from stumbling," and about life after death: "He wipes away every tear." He is a shepherd. Those who stray are like wandering sheep; lost coins and lilies of the field have something to say about our faith and trust.

Along with imagery, short, clear sentences are more likely to capture revelation's meaning. How often have you heard something like this during an Easter liturgy?

Today, my dear brethren, we celebrate the resurrection of our divine Savior, our Blessed Lord, into eternal glory, a profound, salvific event at which those who came to the tomb on that first Easter morning—our Blessed Lady, and that ever-beloved, repentant sinner, Mary Magdalene, and Peter, the first Pope—all were frightened and confused from the past events of Good Friday, but our Lord appeared to them and reassured them with these words, "Do not be afraid."

How about this instead? "Easter. It is dawn. (Pause) Mary, the mother of Jesus and Peter and Mary Magdalene come to the tomb. They are afraid, confused. (Pause) Jesus appears. He is risen! He is calm, confident and reassuring. 'Do not be afraid,' he says."

Each word evokes a picture. Dawn. Peter. Tomb. Afraid. Calm. The words are simple, clean and concise. Listeners can form a picture, as if projected on a screen. Imagination builds as you speak simple words as in a story. The listener can visualize. You, the preacher, build images, one by one, in the minds of your hearers. Pauses are effective too. By pacing your images, give your listeners time to experience both the picture and the emotion.

Image-Maker and Congregation Response

Essentially, then, the preacher is artist and poet. He is also image-maker. His moments in the pulpit are a revealing experience. He joins the many in our society who are part of the "knowledge explosion": in Scripture, technology, film, television, art and design. Marshall McLuhan's thesis is convincing: speech is a cool medium that cries for details to be filled in by the listener. Like other cool media of TV and telephone, it invites audience participation. Listeners have to fill in the blanks. The reader, alone in his room, can be aloof and disinterested. But speech moves toward an instant sensory awareness of the whole picture. As the preacher speaks, the listener moves toward quick responses: "I like what he's saying"; "I'm bored." The listener clicks the preacher on or off in the first few minutes. When reading a novel, a person tends to give the benefit of the doubt to the novelist: the first few chapters are boring, but I'll stick with it, hoping it gets better as the plot develops. The success of a sermon is not in trying to measure how much the listener remembers about it, but what its effect was. Did it move people? Did it give people a sense of God's presence? Did it banish some fear or give hope? Did it get people to say: "You certainly gave me something to think about this week," or "I didn't know that," or "You stirred some feelings in me"?

Conclusion

Long ago, Francis of Assisi pleaded for language in sermons that was "well considered and simple, for the benefit and edification of the people." Augustine, before him, echoed this, as did Vincent de Paul after him. The Council of Trent exhorted priests to speak in a style accommodated to the "capacity of their flocks." Pius XII appealed for "simplicity . . . the word of conviction that comes from the heart and goes to the heart." Pope John XXIII asked preachers to shun "homiletic abstractions and profundities."

The preacher who is unaccustomed to speaking in simple language has a lot of work to do. Without that work he stands in danger of proclaiming theological God-talk, the kind of language that Canon Drinkwater fears "seals off the heart as effectually as trouble in the fusebox shuts off the electric current."

Reading Scripture, studying its words, pondering the daily psalms and readings in the breviary, and imitating the biblical writers' descriptions of persons, places and things will equip the preacher with confidence. Grappling with words and images will become an exercise of joy. The preacher will become a weaver of words that join the mysteries of God.

SPECIFIC POINTS AND EXERCISES FOR STUDY

From POINTS FOR PREPARATION AND DELIVERY (See *Introduction* I)

I. Use direct, clear, and simple language. Keep it concrete. Use image words. Cut out theological or philosophical jargon.

II. Pick out five or six psalms. Write down all the image words. Take three parables and do the same. Read the psalms and parables aloud.

IV. Write an image description of a resurrection experience in your own life. Do the same for a description of the Holy Spirit working in your life.

V. Describe in image words "grace" and "faith."

From EXERCISES AND REFLECTIONS TO ENHANCE PREACHING (See *Introduction* II)

I. Read Scripture for fifteen minutes every day. Try to visualize persons, places, environment of the passage, the inter-relationship of biblical characters with Jesus and each other. Retell out loud, to yourself, what is happening in the passage. Note, especially in the breviary, the strong image and concrete language of the psalms, of the prophets, of Jesus. Study the words used. Write down image words and build up a file on them. Make this Scripture reading *active* reading.

II. When you feel that you've mastered some of the above, start thinking of training people in the parish to be lectors. Build up a core group of public "proclaimers" in the parish. This will enhance their own lives, as well as the faith life of the community.

Keep It Simple

Strike three.
Get your hand off my knee.
You're overdrawn.
Your horse won.
Yes.
No.
You have the account.
Walk.
Don't walk.
Mother's dead.
Basic events
require simple language.
Idiosyncratically euphuistic
eccentricities are the
promulgators of
triturable obfuscation.
What did you do last night?
Enter into a meaningful
romantic involvement
or
fall in love?
What did you have for
breakfast this morning?
The upper part of a hog's
hind leg with two oval
bodies encased in a shell
laid by a female bird
or
ham and eggs?
David Belasco, the great
American theatrical producer,
once said, "If you can't
write your idea on the
back of my calling
card,
you don't have a clear idea."

Reprinted with permission of United Technologies, Box 360, Hartford, Conn. 06141

7.
Some Final Thoughts

ODDS AND ENDS, PET PEEVES AND FUTURE HOPES

To all who want to preach:

Whenever I think of the discipline that goes into preaching—and some of the discouragement that comes from keeping at it—one story in particular comes to mind.

Shortly after the Vatican Council's *Constitution on the Church* was proclaimed, a theological expert recounted some of the behind-the-scenes human tragedy that went into the framing of Council documents.

One world renowned ecclesiologist had presented a working schema based on years of research and scholarship. For many years his insights and publications were respected and widely read. At a meeting of the committee responsible for drafting the Constitution for the Council's vote, this man saw his life's work rejected, tossed aside. His research did not qualify to move the Church in the direction Vatican II had mapped out.

I thought: What a personal tragedy this must have been for that man! The wreckage of years of human toil flipped into a wastebasket. A lifetime's work declared "non grata."

Rewrite and Revise

All analogies limp somewhat, and most of us would be flattering our egos to think that our weekly sermons compare to a theological scholar's years of dedicated research. Yet something of process has to go into sermon preparation. When you decide to spend several hours a week shaping a sermon, you make a commitment to review, rewrite, eliminate, reject, rewrite and begin again. What you thought was a masterpiece of future elocution might, for any number of reasons, need rejection. A good preacher often has to be ruthless with his sermon manuscripts, putting the ax to precious gems which might possibly tickle the ears of his listeners but not move their hearts. Rearrange sections of your sermon that belong better in one place than another. Carry out an intense search for words, images, and simple stories. It is vital, too, that you keep reading over the Scripture texts. Become possessed by them. If one or several paragraphs sound good, and are well written with carefully chosen and honed words, try telling someone else, or telling yourself, what you want to say to test whether you can share that faith without notes. When you can't rephrase, in simple words, what you've written, mainly because you cannot remember what you want to say, it is unlikely that the congregation will remember either. After all, they haven't spent time preparing as you have.

I believe that this little exercise keeps the preacher anchored to his own faith. Some preachers cast their sermons in fancy language found in a book somewhere, or which some other preacher has written. Unless a preacher is highly skilled and adept at public speaking, the material will come out just as it is: someone else's.

Quite often people will tell me that think their priest is using someone else's sermon on Sunday. "It sounds artificial, as if he were just reading words, as if he had no personal commitment to what is on the paper. I really don't think Father ever preaches his own stuff."

You can fool some of the people some of the time. Congregations know when that time is.

Questions, Questions

When writing a sermon, it's a good idea to keep asking yourself questions that subject you to the judgment of honesty: Will this convince those who hear it? Do I believe it? Do I feel possessed by this? Am I excited about what I am saying? Will the congregation be able to grasp this image? Am I using this image because I am impressed with its ability to evoke or because it's a favorite of mine? How strong is the image? What will this word mean to those who hear it?

Can I make this point with an illustration? Is this true? Is it a cliché? How am I like this person whom Jesus meets and talks to? If this had not happened in the life of Jesus or the Bible character, would my life be the same? Would it be different? Has what I am sharing in this sermon made any difference in my own life? Is it empty pious jargon? Does it deal with real life? Or is it abstract? Are the stories about life, or do they merely *speculate* about life?

After you've asked these hard questions, check yourself on your delivery. Keep in mind some of these questions: What's my tone like? Am I patronizing and condescending? Am I posturing, trying to sound pious, puffed up with self-importance, changing my voice into a preachy, churchy style because I have some idea in my head about the way people should sound in a pulpit? Remember: people will pick up any attempt of the preacher to sound different or dramatic, out of style or keeping with what they know him to be in everyday contact. The inflection of the voice or a "pious" stance is not what determines you to be holy. Holiness resides in your character, and people will see through posturing. There is no substitute for a well-trained, rich, resonant, clear, inflected voice, projected in a natural manner. While the preacher combines some of the technical aspects an actor would use, he is not an actor. He is not involved primarily in a dramatic event, though he may use drama. Part of the genius of a good actor is that the listener or viewer is not aware he is acting. The same is true of the preacher. Be yourself—not Fulton Sheen, not William Sloane Coffin, not Martin Luther King, not Jesse Jackson, but just yourself, with all the best gifts, training, discipline and faith that you can muster.

Continue the questions: Do I come across as an alive, warm person or a cold, remote robot delivering an erudite thesis in which my words fail to connect with the live bodies listening in the pews? Am I preaching as sinner to sinner or judge to sinner? As a person chosen by the community to preach the word, or as one apologizing for what I am saying? Am I preaching as an educated person to the ignorant? Am I speaking as spiritual father to the people of God, brother to brother and sister, child of God to child of God?

Am I saying to this group in the pews what I could say to one person, or do the members of the congregation become "them"? Are my words coming off the script so impersonally that they speak to no one? A good rule of thumb here is to pick out someone in the congregation and deliver as if you were speaking directly to that person, engaging him or her, occasionally looking at other areas of the congregation. When you engage one or a few people, then others in the congregation will want to listen, too.

Connections—Engagement

Some preachers believe that they must try to connect visually with everyone, that eye contact with every corner of the church is vital to good communication. Consequently, their head consciously moves from right to left, left to right, up and down. In a sense they are speaking to no one. The example I gave you of fixing on one or a few people is best borne out in your experience with the TV talk shows.

Johnny Carson, Dick Cavett and Merv Griffin speak for fifteen to thirty minutes with one or two people. Only occasionally do they look at the audience. Yet they engage the audience. When they are personally and significantly engaged in conversation with one person, they also are engaging the audience. Have you ever been at a party where there are six, eight, or ten people in a room and two people are engaged in very serious conversation? The others listen and are engaged by it; they listen intently. Mentally and emotionally, they're connected to the two parties. But this quality to engage others presupposes that something is *really* happening between the two people. Some people talk for hours and there is no engagement. They play games with each other but say nothing. It's all on the surface. There is no intention to communicate. Others talk for five minutes and it's a significant, human encounter. Something serious has happened. Values are questioned, directions are challenged, emotional juices are flowing, depth is shared. Which category is yours?

How Long?

And now, for the length of the sermon. One minute commercials and half-hour to two-hour programs bombard Americans daily on TV. We are accustomed to getting the message quickly, and well! Our concentration span is short. Even when we have watched a sporting event such as football or soccer, an instant replay helps us to avoid thinking through what has happened. Commercials give us relief from the tension of concentration—a chance to get a beer, to check the oven temperature, or to voice an opinion to a sympathetic ear.

Daily media such as this can't help but affect our attitudes toward listening to one person for any length of time, especially when there is no visual component. "Keep it short, Father," is a response both to the kind of culture we're in as well as to the Catholic's way of telling the preacher that "keeping it short" will rescue him from the mediocre pulpit fare he's been served for so long. It's a curious fact that Catholics, in pre-Vatican Council days, accustomed to long sermons at weekly missions and occasional Sunday sermons, weren't nearly as critical as they are now. Their expectations have changed with and in a visual culture. Those expectations are higher, too, in regard to quality.

It has been my experience that daily homilies of three to five minutes are acceptable provided that they are well thought out and leave the listener with one clear point—a "developed thought," as someone has called them. Most people who go to daily Mass appreciate a comment on the Scriptures, some practical application to their lives.

As for Sunday sermons, it has been my impression that congregations welcome an organized, well-delivered sermon which speaks to their experience and leaves them richer in faith. They are also prepared to spend ten to fifteen minutes, or even longer, listening, provided they feel that the preacher is prepared, takes them seriously and speaks to them personally. Within the Protestant tradition, the sermon has been central to worship, and voluntary congregations continue to flock on Sundays to hear sermons that last as long as three-quarters of an hour. The Catholic has no such tradition. He will sit through a parade of symbols—incense, chant, processions, ritual—but not sermons. I personally feel, though, that Catholics are crying for good preaching. When they hear it, they'll tolerate reasonable length and be grateful when they feel engaged. When preaching renews itself, some people may return to the Church. It's good to have a limit in mind and to be disciplined in time. The more important value is for the preacher to insure connections between himself and the congregation. When this is really happening, time becomes relative—like a good talk with a friend—and the congregation isn't conscious of how long the preacher has been in the pulpit. When preaching improves, admonitions such as "Keep it short, Father" or "The best sermon is no sermon" will begin to fade.

Language—Jargon

This leads us to language in the pulpit. Cultural emphasis on personalism and therapeutic aids and skills in the past decade have, in some cases, converted the pulpit into an arena where the preacher works out his own problems on the congregation. Many young preachers have had seminary formation in which group process, using a therapeutic model, has been central. The value of this model has proven itself in helping the seminarian to establish trusting relationships with supervisors, members of the group or another person. The therapeutic/group process has its own language, its own rules, its own symbols of communication, its own internal dynamic. For those not accustomed to this model (which means most of the congregation) the language and method can appear esoteric. Some of it gets mixed up with the jargon of the counter-culture and has been laundered up for the Church and hardened into a language movement which has lost the relationship to people's experience. This private language distances the preacher from the people and fixes and separates more firmly whatever separate worlds they live in. The pulpit needs language which builds communication bonds.

The use of private language is not always intentional or conscious, but is often supported by the culture in which we live. Maudlin and narcissistic soul-baring on the part of the preacher manipulates the congregation into feeling sorry for him. The listener, who comes to church to be fed the word, finds himself in a reverse ministerial role. Rather than feeling free to accept the preacher's ministry to them, congregations now feel that it is they who must minister to the hurting preacher.

This is a delicate area, obviously. Sometimes a fine line exists between ministering and being ministered to. Many former functions and expectations of religion have become pre-empted by counseling and therapy, with its own promises and guarantees of salvation and healing. The therapist or group leader is the high priest of salvation. The preacher is part of a distinctly different forum than the therapy group, and it is important to safeguard the autonomy and historical prerogatives of the pulpit. Preaching is a distinct and unique form of communication and has its own inner integrities. The process method, familiar to counseling and group forums, can help people to feel whole again; at the same time this methodology can make authentic proclamation difficult because process tends to emphasize what is tentative and becoming, while preaching presumes a message to be handed down, a statement of what Jesus has done to and for us. Preaching invites an affirmation and an Amen to what is shared. It is proclaimed to evoke a response.

Personal Experiences Shared

Related to the use of therapeutic language in the pulpit is the way in which a preacher shares his own personal experiences in the sermon. Since personal faith is an essential element of preaching, it is a good idea, at this point, to say something about the ways in which a preacher draws on personal experience.

We know it is possible to draw on personal experiences in the preaching forum and say little or nothing about God. In my teaching experience I have heard students deliver entire sermons without any reference to faith, God, or the mediation of Jesus in their own or the congregation's lives. In preaching, the emphasis is on speaking *through* an experience. The experience filters the way in which God has spoken in our lives. In a group or counseling session, an experience is often recounted through raw emotion, often supported by unvarnished feelings. This is acceptable to achieve the aim of therapy or group process. Other people in the group are encouraged to respond and give their own insights—to state how they feel about what the person has said or done. This is a different forum than the pulpit, even though both the pulpit and the group may be dealing with a person's deepest pain, faith or hope. In preaching the purpose is to instill a sense of praise and thanksgiving in the congregation. It is to make some God-sense out of what has happened in both your lives—yours and the congregation's. One's own hurt and pain, joy and hope can be, and often is, a means of discovering God, but they cannot be the focal point of the sermon lest the sermon become maudlin acting-out. One's experience shared from the pulpit can only be a springboard to the good news. Centering too much on the preacher's own problems and pain places the congregation at a disadvantage because the preacher exclusively centers on himself and not on those who have come to be fed the word of God.

Some students—and ordained preachers—would spend a third of the sermon time telling the congregation how many hours they had anguished over what they would say, how many walks alone in the woods and on the seashore pondering how and what God wanted them to say, and how many hours they had prayed over their sermon. The congregation is not interested in the anguish that preceded the pulpit moment. They want the preacher to get to the point. "Tell me, Father, what's the good news?"

"I" centered preaching often degenerates into maudlin sentimentality and inappropriate bad taste in a public forum such as the pulpit. This is embarrassing to the congregation. The pulpit is a focal point of ministering and caring for the people at that specific faith moment, and the preacher's skill and faith should prevent it from becoming a therapeutic instrument for his own needs.

Let me give you an example. I once heard a priest say something like this from the pulpit to a crowded congregation: "I'm really not prepared to talk about this Gospel today because I'm all mixed up emotionally. Last night I received the bad news that I wasn't accepted for a graduate program and this has shattered all my expectations. I'm really hurting today. . . . "

And on and on he went, with his pain pouring out. However sympathetic one might have been with the poor fellow, the pulpit was not the forum for ministering to his personal needs. There was no proclamation there.

The reverse happened in another pastoral moment. Not long ago I listened to a priest speak on grief and the healing power of God's grace when loss grips our lives. The occasion was a funeral, and the sermon was powerful. I did not know anything about the priest's life, but I could feel the strength, depth and caring of his words permeate the congregation. His strength became my strength. His hope transferred itself into the hearts of the bereaved sitting in the congregation. It was obvious that this priest had gone to the well and drunk deeply of living waters at some time of utter grief in his own life. He could not have spoken so sensitively had his own faith not been tested and found strong. But not once did he speak of, or refer to, any personal grief or tragedy in his own life. We knew, though, that he had experienced it deeply. This was the unspoken message that reached my heart and my gut. Only later did I find out that he had recently lost both parents, a younger brother from leukemia, and a sister in a tragic accident. From his own personal grief he responded to the grief of those in the pews, *to whom he was called, at that moment, to minister*, and he healed their emotional brokenness. They received and cherished the grace and graciousness of his ministry to them. God's presence was proclaimed and felt.

While teaching homiletics, I have heard students deliver sermons which borrow heavily from the excessive personalistic jargon born out of the sensitivity cults of the 1960's. It is not uncommon today for sermons to be peppered with language about "growing fully human," "to be fully myself, as Jesus was fully himself," being "freed up by the Gospel to be my best me," "loving the 'I' in myself," "plugging into the creative possibilities that my personhood triggers for me as I interface with someone else's love," et cetera, ad infinitum. It's a case of a new jargon replacing an old one. We used to parody some of the old pulpit language as cliché—"Holy Mother Church," "my dearly beloved people," "under the pain of mortal sin," and a whole assortment of ecclesiastical fare. There's no substitute for the good, clear, strong language found in the Bible. You can't go wrong with that.

Gimmicks

Along with in-group language are the pulpit gimmicks. I agree that visual aids and attention getters in preaching can be effective. They must be used well, however, and presented with skill and imagination. Most often they draw too much attention to the preacher who is trying to be avant garde or different. Most of the ones I've seen fall flat.

The irony is that most of the gimmickry comes at a time when the educational level of Catholics is at an all-time high. People are accustomed to seeing real pros on TV and in the movies. They can easily spot the contrived, the artificial, and are usually turned off by it. Any liturgy in which preaching is too reliant on multi-media or theatrics is almost bound to fail. The pastoral minister is not trained in dramatic communication. Good drama, the coordination of stage effects, the use of media and visual aids—all these require professional training and expertise. They are not something that can be used casually. You have only to look at the toil and sweat that goes into a play or musical presentation—months of rehearsal and coordination—to get an idea of what is working against the preacher or liturgist who tries to do this weekly or even monthly. Most of them are productions, not faith events.

Nelson Logal (writing in *Homiletic and Pastoral Review*) believes that the explanation for so much gimmickry in the pulpit is due to fatalism in priests about the effectiveness of preaching in general. This convinces them not to try to preach well but to rely on canned sermons and other aids. When gimmicks are used, the trick often becomes the message, and one is more aware of the preacher stretching to be relevant than of God's action in his life. The prevailing cultural climate of the age centers on pop, electronic and high decibel noise.

One writer put it well when he said: "The tricks of the trade can be quite serviceable when they are used discriminatingly as servants of the word, but they have a tendency to harden into dead stylizations when they take on the characteristics of a preaching manner. When they are not properly concealed and when they become habitual they tend to trivialize and even to debase effective communication in the pulpit. In an hour when we should be fighting for the future, we tend to fiddle away evangelization time on Sunday with cute tricks and self-serving devices which make us appear to be 'tinkling cymbals and sounding brass.' "

Nuff said!

"Lettuce" sermons

There is no substitute, then, for a sound theology, cast into human words and images, to evoke a positive, unconditional response from persons who have experienced God's love. One does not need gadgets and theatrics to show this. A strong belief in the power of God to move hearts will help us to avoid what teachers of homiletics call "lettuce" sermons: "Let us now do this or that" or "Let us be resolved today to . . ." or "Now that we have tasted God's goodness in his word, let us . . ."

There's nothing wrong in this, of course, but it has become one more cliché, one more untidy device. It is as if the preacher believes that he can evoke response by a final or frequent exhortation to "let us" do this or that. It's enough to say here that it's a good idea for the student of homiletics and the preacher to avoid the "lettuce" clauses in favor of a different appeal to the congregation.

"If" clauses

Stay away, too, from the "if" clauses in your preaching—for example, "If you do this, God will reward you," "If you do this, God will forgive you," "If you go to Communion, you will become good."

There's a sense in which an "if" clause has a kernel of truth. The problem is that an "if" clause sounds neo-Pelagian: "If I work hard enough, God will reward me." It places the emphasis on me and not on God. "If" clauses border on dangerous (and often heretical) theological presuppositions. "If" motivates in the wrong direction: "If you don't go to Mass, you'll go to hell."

The basic Christian teaching is that God's love is gratuitous. Nothing we do earns it. God gives it freely. Jesus' death on the cross gives us forgiveness of our sins and opens the way to the Father. We open ourselves in and to that gift of faith and respond with a life of faith. This faith includes good works. As we believe that the Lord has done these things to and for us, our response is one of faith to that same Lord. God gives freely; it is not *quid pro quo*. The latecomer to the vineyard receives the same reward as those who worked all day long; Mary Magdalene was forgiven gratuitously and not in return for a promise that she would sin no more. Presumably her experience of forgiveness converted her into a more faithful person, and a new kind of life grew out of that forgiveness. She changed her life *because* she was forgiven. When the preacher communicates this kind of love and friendship as it is revealed in God through Jesus, there's no end to the possibilities which exist to convert the hearts of his listeners. This is to be paramount in the preacher's mind.

The problem with the "if" and "when" clauses is that they leave the listener with the impression that "if" and "when" we do certain things, God will love us, and "if" and "when" we don't do them, God won't love us. This places Pelagianism over God's gratuitous love. So many "if's" cloud authentic Catholic teaching yet are standard pulpit fare. We can understand why because the conditional "if" governs so many of our daily experiences. "If you get all A's on your report card or if you make Little League or win this or that prize, we'll love you," or "If you're good, God will love you." For the many people who do not believe in their essential goodness and have trouble believing that they are lovable (many religious people suffer from this), it is crucial that the pulpit be a platform where God's love is proclaimed unconditionally. That itself will lead to love, faith, hope, and morality. People will come to believe in themselves. Their response will be a lived faith. "If" clauses reveal more the preacher's attitudes about God than what they exhort the congregation to accomplish. The preacher cannot proclaim often and loudly enough the essential message of Jesus: you are forgiven, always, when you don't deserve it; Jesus' love and forgiveness are extravagant, radical, without anger, without negotiation, with no "if's", "and's" or "but's" attached, without accounts, without balance sheets, without debits. Religion links our experience of being forgiven and loved with God's forgiveness and love. Once it is proclaimed enough from our pulpits and becomes the basic message of evangelization, how one lives and loves and believes after this proclamation will not need moral exhortations.

The other side of the coin is similar: preach what God has done for us. The congregation wants to hear what God has done for and to them. Some preachers spend their time in the pulpit telling the people all the bad things they have done to God, what they "must," "should," and "ought to" do. There's not an iota of good news about God's saving action in their lives. Yet the preacher's purpose is to show how God breaks into our lives. We are saved by God's actions, not our own. The preacher is there to help us see God's loving actions in all the moments of our lives. He is there to call forth our ordinary experiences and memories of grace to help us discover new possibilities of meaning and understanding in our lives. The preacher is there to lead his listener to have a heart that is more forgiving, trustworthy, steadfast, faithful, and compassionate in imitation of God the Father in Jesus. Through his own reflection and prayer on the revealed word, the preacher has a vocation to say what you "know" more and better than what you know and to open new paths toward what you do not know. The preacher seeks to translate the idealism of the congregation into words, to come out of the book of life. Like the musician who puts his experiences and vision to music, the preacher gives form to his faith. We can do this only when we feel that God is near. The preacher's words are given to feed, nourish and strengthen the faith that has already led the congregation to the church. His words are to caress their hearts so that their hearts can be changed. Through him, God gives power for life. The hearer's response will be a conversion toward love, hope, prayer, contemplation, a sense of the sacred, faith, good works, forgiveness, compassion and nourishment of one another's faith. Through the preacher's words we come to believe more earnestly that goodness is more ultimate than "un-good."

Finally I share both a hope and an appeal. Whenever I read about efforts at evangelization I wonder how this will be brought about without a massive renewal of preaching. We can spend millions of dollars on communication for evangelization and applaud the efforts of those who evangelize. When all is said and done, the pulpit remains the basic instrument and place of evangelization. "To announce the word" must happen there, first and foremost. When preaching is renewed and taken as seriously as is Canon Law, fund raising, and endless committee meetings, then evangelization will happen.

In my wild moments of dreaming, I envision and hope for the day when bishops will raise a million-or-so dollars to set up preaching institutes around the country. I look for the day when they will urge, exhort, encourage, subsidize—use whatever legitimate means possible—to get priests, sisters, and laypeople who wish to proclaim and preach to attend them before preaching faculties for priests and deacons and permissions for others are given. I look to the day when every priest who enrolls in continuing education will take a course on preaching or communication skills.

This sounds like a radical solution, but only radical because preaching, sad to say, is still the stepchild of pastoral ministry. Despite noble documents to the contrary, it continues to hold low priority in the pastoral ministry of the Church. For the health of Catholicism and the work of evangelization, the renewal of proclamation and preaching, as an art, a skill and a command of Jesus, is an urgent task.

My last words are pragmatic. I urge you to insist, whenever possible, on training and professionalism in the proclamation of Scripture at daily and Sunday liturgies. In my travels around the country I am always astounded at how little attention has been given to this critical pastoral need. Celebrants continue to pick someone casually from the congregation to proclaim the Scriptures. Lectors read badly; they cannot be heard, do not know how to use a microphone, mispronounce words, and lack emphasis, life and spirit in their reading and pronunciation. This happens at weddings, funerals, baptisms—wherever congregations gather. It is quite impossible for anyone to be an active listener when he or she cannot shape images out of the words which are heard. Stories of Jesus were dynamic, live events. There was excitement, conflict, enthusiasm, wonder, fear, and exhilaration. People were raised up from the dead! To capture these lived moments from the lethargy seen and heard in our pulpits would require divine intervention.

It sounds heavyhanded, I suppose, to insist on this kind of training in proclamation. At the same time it is certain that the liturgy of the word will remain in its present state of limbo if attitudes and initiatives remain the same. Reading and proclaiming in a public forum is a skill to be learned. People need to be trained. It does not seem too much to expect the same kind of professionalism and quality from our ministers (clerical and lay) that we expect in the medical, legal and teaching professions. To be faced, week after week, with mediocrity in the liturgy of the word can only create indifference to Sacred Scripture and erode the faith of the people. The word of God is too precious an ointment to be poured out so carelessly.

Massive commitment is needed to reverse this trend at the liturgy of the word—to tap the good will and generosity of laypersons who would gladly participate in training programs when given leadership by priests who are first and foremost responsible for the quality of the liturgy in their parishes. It is a great challenge to a noble work.

It is in this way that the believing community will open its ears to the word of the Lord and be made strong and whole.

SPECIFIC POINTS AND EXERCISES FOR STUDY

From POINTS OF PREPARATION AND DELIVERY (See *Introduction* I).

I. Meditate, Reflect, Pray.
   (a) Take the stories, memories, exegesis, and events of the week and reflect on the ways in which God met you in them. Make some of this the focus of your daily and weekly meditation and reflection.
   (b) How do these Scripture passages reflect, similarly, the ways in which God reveals himself to you today—heals, forgives you, is your light, raises you up, etc.?

II. Write/Rewrite.
   (a) Develop the sermon. Move from outline to prose development. Keep asking: Could I say this more simply? With more imagery? Review, rewrite, cut. "The wastebasket is the writer's best friend." Cut—even if it means parting with a gem. Ask: Does this sentence or word hinder or help my sermon? Remember: attention not won in the first couple of minutes is never won at all.
   (b) Get rid of the "if's," "let us," "shoulds" and "oughts."

III. Conclusion.
   (a) Know it well. Concentrate on it. A bad conclusion can ruin a good sermon. Beautiful structures of words and ideas collapse around bad conclusions.
   (b) Relate the conclusion to the beginning. Bring the congregation back to your opening. Summarize and exhort, offering practical applications.

IV. Write a five hundred word essay describing your personal theology/philosophy of preaching.

 V. Design a training program for lectors. See *A Handbook for Lectors* by William M. Carr, Paulist Press, 1968. Begin to take initiatives to improve public proclamation in your parish, community or seminary.

Appendices

A.
Preaching Course or Workshop

A MODEL

Various options exist for teaching homiletics in a one semester time-span or two or three workshops. This one presumes a semester, with two hours each week. It is an introduction mainly for those who have never preached.

Goals of the Course

- Principles of communication
- Scriptural communication and proclamation
- Some principles of clear, concise, image composition
- Delivery
- Self-critique
- Critique from the listener/congregation
- Concrete ways to implement feedback/critique in preparation and delivery of the next homily

Frequency of Delivery

Each student will make a weekly presentation. This will consist of (1) proclamation of Scripture and/or (2) delivery of a homily. Critique will follow.

Course Requirements

- Preparation of Scripture passage for proclamation: emphasis on key words in the passage, voice and tone variation, sense of drama in the proclamation
- Writing and delivery of homilies
- Video-taping of each student delivering a homily, with critique of body movement, gestures, delivery
- Five hundred word essay on student's theology/philosophy of preaching
- Book report on any of the books in the bibliography with prior consultation with the instructor
- Midterm self-evaluation of student's progress, areas for growth and development of strengths
- A ten to fifteen minute didactic given every other week by instructor; these will be homiletic helps based on theory, experience, congregational reaction, etc.; some of this can be integrated into the individual critiques when specific points made to one individual are applicable generally to all
- End of semester evaluation (verbal and written)

Course Outline (Based on two hour sessions)

1. Introduction of class participants (students stand up in front of the group to do this). Statement of personal goals in the course. Explanation of course components and requirements.

2. Extemporaneous/impromptu talks of two to three minutes. Each student will draw a card with a topic written on it. He is given two minutes alone to organize his thought. He returns to deliver the talk. The members of the congregation, not told about the topic, share with him in their critique whether they could determine the topic by the focus of his remarks. This exercise is given to help the student think on his feet, organize his thoughts quickly and coherently, develop confidence and work at a clear focus of presentation. Instructor gives about twenty minutes of communication theory: practical hints and helps.

3. Each student chooses a Scripture passage which is a personal

favorite, proclaims it to the class, and tells "why" it means something to his faith, drawing on personal experience. (3 to 4 minutes)

4. Homily preparation: construct a homily together in class based on *Ten Points for Preparation and Delivery of Sermons* (see Introduction I). Instructor leads class, taking them through the steps. The Scripture passage to be used will have been given out the former week to allow for reflection, exegesis, jottings etc. Emphasis will be directed toward clarity of writing, image words, examples, practical points to be made for the congregation, strong conclusion.

5. Preach the homily prepared in (4) above. Half the class preaches. (5–7 minutes)

6. Same as (5) above.

7. Preach on readings of following Sunday. Video-tape. Each student will bring to class an audio cassette to include himself proclaiming the Scripture passage. For the remainder of the course, homilies to be maximum of 7 minutes. Half the class preaches each week.

8. Same as (7).

9. Midterm evaluation. General class/group evaluation. If this group feels it is too early in the course for this, adjust date.

10. Scriptures of the following Sunday. Video-tape.

11. Preach on the topic of parish renewal.

12. Same as (11). (Turn in 500 word essays on preaching.)

13. Topic: Advent, Thanksgiving, Christmas (when course is taught in fall semester. Video-tape.

14. Same as (13).

15. Loneliness or Alcoholism. Show your pastoral concern in a homily.

16. Same as (15).

17. Final homily. My preference is not to emphasize this much more than any of the others. It should be treated more as one more sermon than a "final examination."

18. Class critique. Schedule appointments for private meetings, etc.

Students are to hand in written sermons or outlines each week. Instructor will read, comment and return. Sometimes students will be asked to rewrite sermons with specific goals in mind: image words, shorter, more concise sentences, better use of Scripture, imagination, writing without using any philosophical, abstract words. These are particularly good exercises to help students think concretely for preaching purposes.

Proclamation Component of a Preaching Course

Some time will be spent in critiquing the student's reading and proclamation of the Scriptures. Simple things will be considered, such as *pausing* before the reading of the Epistle or Gospel so that the noise level in the church decreases as people get settled (sitting down from standing before the Epistle or standing for the Gospel from a sitting position). This allows the people time to focus attention for the next event. It sounds almost too self-evident to mention, but my experience is that readers (clergy and laypersons alike) dive right into the readings and sermons without any interval of space to allow the people to get settled and quieted down, and to develop a new direction in their attention. Pausing is a simple communication skill often ignored. It is almost impossible, psychologically, for a congregation to switch immediately from hearing the Gospel from a standing position to giving attention to the preacher after sitting down without some pause for focus and attention.

Bad Habits of Proclamation

Some bad reading and proclamation habits are creeping into the word service. The simple conclusion "This is the Word of the Lord" is given for the readings from the Old Testament and the Epistles. "This is the Gospel of the Lord" is given as a conclusion to the Gospel. I hear all sorts of variations, with conjunctions like "and," as well as additions such as "My dear people, brothers and sisters, this is the Gospel (Word) of the Lord. . . . " etc.

No need to nitpick, but from the point of view of communication there's no good reason to depart from simple forms. First of all, the end of the reading or Gospel does not call for the conjunction "and." It's bad grammar. Between the last word of the reading and the statement "This is the Word (Gospel) of the Lord," only a moment of silence is needed, followed by, simply, "This is the Word of the Lord." "This is the Gospel of the Lord."

Remember this as a rule of thumb. Congregations accustomed to responding in a certain way at various points in the liturgy (responses which are familiar, learned and almost instinctive) will be thrown off when the leader introduces new and unfamiliar words. The framework for dialogue and communication—word and response so necessary to good liturgy—is weakened or destroyed. The liturgy has evolved and developed into a delicate balance between the priest's words and the congregation's response, a rhythm which continues through the Mass from the greeting to the final blessing. Improvisation at these key parts of the Mass rarely enhances worship in the Roman Rite.

B.
Advanced Preaching

A MODEL

Unless a student begins his preaching courses in a department which has a common curriculum, it cannot be presumed that basic theory of communication has been taught. In any case, the first class should be spent reviewing communication theories and practice, breathing and relaxation exercises, and points for preparation of sermons noted in the Introduction of this book.

Advanced preaching courses can begin to introduce the student to specialized preaching which he will have to do as a pastoral minister. If possible, each student may arrange to preach in a parish with selected members of the congregation critiquing him. In one advanced preaching course which I taught, the sisters at Trinity College invited a student to preach once a week, followed by lunch and a critiquing group of about five sisters. It was especially helpful to have women responding to some of the presuppositions and language of male preachers.

In preaching on any of the topics listed below, the student should keep in mind the importance of developing images to match the symbols and images which the Church and Scripture use in the celebration of the sacraments. A clear theme can be developed with each sacrament.

Sacraments

Baptism: life and faith-community

Eucharist: food, being fed, comm-union
Penance: forgiveness from the past/called to the future; resurrection
Confirmation: gifts of the Spirit/living an adult faith
Marriage: commitment
Holy Orders/Profession into Religious Life: service/commitment
Anointing of the Sick: healing of body and spirit, hope, Jesus being close to us in our infirmity, etc. For Wakes/Funerals: articulate the grief of the people briefly and then move on to hope, a new kind of life in Jesus

Preaching to Persons in Various Situations

Children: develop images in your sermon to children; caution: do not talk down to them or patronize, since children pick up that attitude immediately
Teenagers
College students
College professors on retreat
Women
Elderly
Homebound/Shut-ins
Prisoners
Alcoholics
Emotionally disturbed persons
Drug-addicted persons
Sermon in sign language when possible

Doctrinal

Trinity
God the Father
God the Son
God the Holy Spirit
Heaven
Hell
Purgatory
Limbo
Death

Church
Grace
Sin
Bible
Pope
Ecumenism
Liturgy
Sexuality
Morality
Mary
Saints

Liturgical Cycle Topics

Advent
Immaculate Conception
Christmas
Presentation of Jesus in the Temple
Epiphany
Ash Wednesday
Lent
Good Friday
Easter/Resurrection
Ascension
Pentecost
Trinity Sunday
Transfiguration
Assumption
All Saints
All Souls
Immaculate Conception

Parish Life—Universal Church

Parish renewal (preaching a persuasive sermon to increase participation in parish education-social programs).
Social justice (poverty, involvement in political affairs etc.).

Money appeals: stewardship, charities, support of schools and seminaries, elderly priests and sisters, for nursing homes, diocesan institutions.

Appeals to help in liturgy: extraordinary ministers, lectors, parish committees, choir, music groups etc.

Preaching on topics such as parish life can be good practice for later ministry when the priest's power of persuasion is critical to pastoral leadership.

Last but not least, I try to ask each student to deliver one sermon in which he consciously uses humor in good taste.

C.
Sermon Construction Aids*

All sermons can include these basic ingredients:

Introduction.

Topic. What do you want to preach about? Have this clearly in your mind.

Objective.

What do you want to accomplish? One clear goal. "No matter how well prepared a sermon is, if it isn't said well and presented properly, you will not accomplish your objective." "It's not *what* he said; it's *how* he said it."

Message.

Attention getter: story, personal experience, question. "Ho-Hum Crasher or Ho-Hum Snore."

Development of Message. Illustrative Examples.

Stories, anecdotes, facts, statistics, authorities, humor chosen to support your objective. Keep building, as a stone mason uses bricks to build a house. Keep them short, clear, concise, with momentum in

---

* Based on the Borden and Busse Formula of Communication.

pace and image. Keep them uncluttered. Use pauses for emphasis between "for instances."

Practical Application.

"So what? What about me? What do I do about it?" Your development above should start the congregation wondering what the point is for them.

Application.

Give them an answer to their questions: "So what's in this for me?" Give some practical help to live out the Gospel message. Reassure them, strengthen them with hope. Move them from message to practice.

Conclusion.

Keep it short, concise, clear. Returning to the beginning as a link to your introductory remarks, which presumably they remember, is a good idea.

D.
Some Basic Readings
for an Introductory Course
in Preaching

Books and Articles

Babin, David E., *Week In—Week Out: A New Look at Liturgical Preaching.* The Seabury Press, 1976.

Burke, John, O.P., *Gospel Power: Toward the Revitalization of Preaching.* Alba House, 1978.

Carr, William M. *A Handbook for Lectors,* Paulist Press, 1968.

Crum, Milton, *Manual on Preaching,* Judson Press, 1970. (Read especially his material on morality sermons, pp. 17–18, 20–21, 37–38, 73–74, and 117ff.)

Graham, William, "A Personal Approach to Preaching," *Preaching Today* (A Journal of Homiletics), Vol. 3, No. 3, 1968.

Murphy, David M., "Inductive Preaching: Reaching People Where They Are," *The Priest,* June 1978, pp. 11–14.

Nouwen, Henri J., *Creative Ministry.* Doubleday and Co., Inc., 1971. (Read especially his section on preaching.)

Pennington, Chester, *God Has a Communication Problem: Creative Preaching Today.* Hawthorne Books, Inc., 1976.

Thompson, W. D., "Testing the Audience Analysis Skills of Ministers," *Preaching* IV (May-June, 1969), pp. 1–7.

Encyclopedia Articles

"Preaching (Homiletic Theory)," *The New Catholic Encyclopedia,* McGraw-Hill, 1967, Vol. II, pp. 690ff.

"Theology of Preaching," *The New Catholic Encyclopedia,* McGraw-Hill, 1967, Vol. II, pp. 697ff.

Documents of Vatican II
Dogmatic Constitution on Divine Revelation *(Dei Verbum)*—chapters 2 and 6.
Constitution on the Sacred Liturgy *(Sacrosanctum Concilium)*—chapters 1 (sections I and II) and 2.
Decree on the Bishops' Pastoral Office in the Church *(Christus Dominus)*—chapter 2.
Dogmatic Constitution on the Church *(Lumen Gentium)*—chapter 3.
Decree on the Ministry and Life of Priests *(Presbyterorum Ordinis)*—chapters 1, 2 (section I) and 3 (section I)

Books on Writing and Expression

Dillon, David, *Writing Experience and Expression,* D. C. Heath and Co., 1976.
Strunk, W., Jr., and E. B. White, *The Elements of Style.* Macmillan, 1972.

E.
Sermon Critique

PROPOSED FORM

Preacher―――――――――――――――

Text-Topic――――――――――――――

Rating of Sermon on 1–5 scale:
5   Excellent. *Wow! Great!*
4   Good. Really worth listening to.
3   Average. It's O.K. but it won't move many people. Some yawns.
2   Below average. Pretty bad. Wish he'd wind it up and sit down.
1   Poor. I should have stayed home!

A. Content

1. Biblical Fidelity: Accurate interpretation of text? Exegesis? Stayed with text during the sermon?

2. Theological Integrity: Soundness of doctrinal assumptions? Fidelity to traditional understanding of Church on this subject? Good explanation of changes of interpretation due to doctrinal development, etc.?

3. Real: Does it touch actual life of the people?

4. Imaginative Power: Adequacy and authenticity of images, stories, illustrations?

5. Personal Experience: Good proportion to use of Scripture and other material? Focus on God or self?

B. Structure

1. Introduction: Attention-getters. Real? Contrived? Too Long? Ho-hum crashers?

2. Focus: Clarity of major idea? Fidelity to development of idea with clarity?

3. Progression: Pace? Movement? Development of thought? Transitions? Drama?

4. Language: Simplicity? Image? Theoretical? Heady? Intellectual? Active voice? Cliché? Church-pious?

5. Conclusion: Sufficient? Prepared? Any relationship to opening image or story?

C. Delivery

1. Voice: Volume? Quality? Pitch naturalness? Enunciation of words?

2. Vocal Style: Inflectional pattern? Monotone? Lack of enthusiasm? Passive? Dynamic? Energetic?

3. Body Language: Stance? Posture? Gestures? Facial expression? Relaxed? Stiff? Indifferent? Appearance, dress etc.?

4. Eye Contact: Focus? Movement?

5. Other not mentioned above (hands in pockets, holding onto pulpit, etc.

D. General

1. In one sentence, what do you think was the aim or goal of the sermon? What was the main point?

2. What was the balance between "Law" and "Gospel" in the sermon? What was the good news?

3. What basic attitude or emotion toward the congregation did the preacher project? Pastoral? Understanding? Caring? Authoritarian? Moralistic?

4. Did you get the impression he believed what he was saying?

5. What was the chief impact of this sermon on you? Apart from acting as a intellectual critic, what was your "gut" reaction during the sermon? Your feelings?

6. What was the major strength(s) of the sermon?

7. What was its major weakness(es)?

8. What would you like to see this person do to strengthen and improve his preaching?

In the opening classes, it is important to discuss the importance of honesty in feedback. Critiquing is often difficult for anyone to receive. When the critiques are cloaked in overly sensitive language, or everyone is walking on eggs to guard against hurt feelings, little progress is made. Critiquing is an art, and there should be constructive development. Sometimes the best service to the student or preacher is to say: "Your sermon was bad, unprepared, badly delivered." Better to hear this in class than after ordination, which, sadly enough, is often never to hear it at all.

Suggestion: ask priests, fellow seminarians, and parishioners to critique your sermons. An effective learning experience is to pick out five or six persons of varying age, education, interests, etc. to critique your sermons on Sunday and to give you feedback, collectively or individually. This can be a great source of support and growth pastorally and spiritually. It is also a good way to experience shared responsibility and accountability to one another in a parish community. (See Appendix F: *A Form for Parishioners to Use in Critiquing the Preacher.*

F.
A Form for Parishioners to Use in Critiquing the Preacher*

Proclaiming the Word of God

"For the priest to renew his service to the Word of God, he needs to continually renew his understanding of that Word."

"For since no one can be saved who has not first believed, it is the first task of priests as co-workers of the bishops to preach the Gospel of God to all men."

"Some elements of preparation are indispensable. The opportunity to reflect intimately on the community is essential, with a sensitivity to their needs, compassion toward their struggles and awareness of the cultural, economic and social forces which influence them."

"Among steps taken by priests to improve preaching: receiving a reaction from the people on a formal and regular basis."

1. PREACHING (1 is lowest rank; 6 is highest)
   Relative Importance to You 1 2 3 4 5 6
   Effectiveness of the Pastor 1 2 3 4 5 6
   No Basis for Judgment 0

* Reprinted with permission of Rev. Thomas Culhane, Pastor, Most Pure Heart of Mary Church, Topeka, Kansas.

2. Which of the following would best describe your attitude toward Father's preaching?

_____ I look forward to it.   _____ I wish there wasn't any.
_____ I just tolerate it.
_____ I feel neutral about it. _____ My feeling varies.

3. When preaching to you, do you feel he is. . . . .
_____ talking to you on your level?
_____ talking above your head?
_____ talking down to you as a child?

4. Does his preaching . . .
   A. help you better know Christ?

   _____ Always   _____ Sometimes
   _____ Often   _____ Never

   B. give you something practical for your daily life?

   _____ Always   _____ Sometimes
   _____ Often   _____ Never

   C. give you a better understanding of your faith in the world today?

   _____ Always   _____ Sometimes
   _____ Often   _____ Never

   D. indicate compassion and sensitivity to the needs of the people of this parish?

   _____ Always   _____ Sometimes
   _____ Often   _____ Never

   E. move you to lead a more Christian life?

   _____ Always   _____ Sometimes
   _____ Often   _____ Never

F. give you new food for thought and prayer?

_____ Always   _____ Sometimes
_____ Often   _____ Never

5. Do you think Father's homilies are

_____ well-prepared?
_____ unprepared?
_____ partially prepared?

6. How does the way Father preaches *sound* to you? (Check as many as apply.)

_____ natural
_____ angry
_____ inspiring
_____ involved in what he's saying
_____ enthusiastic
_____ recited
_____ sincere
_____ friendly
_____ monotoned
_____ indifferent or bored
_____ other

7. Does the sound system in our church help you to hear Father well enough?

_____ yes
_____ no

8. What does Father usually preach about? (Open-ended question)

_____
_____
_____

A. Do you find it meaningful to you?

_____ yes
_____ no

9. What would *you* like to hear preached about?
   (Open-ended question)

   _____

   _____

   _____

10. What do you think should not be preached about?
    (Open-ended question)

    _____

    _____

    _____

11. What would be one, two, or three main suggestions you would like to make to Father today to help him in his preaching?
    (Open-ended question)

    _____

    _____

    _____

12. In what age grouping would you be placed?

    Under 21 _____   21 to 30 _____

    30 to 40 _____   40 to 50 _____

    50 to 65 _____   65 or over _____

Comments: _____

_____

_____

"Priestly ministry is not a finished reality, a fully achieved art. Neither is it something frail, a fragile object unable to withstand the taxing passage through change and time. Rather, what the sources of faith and theology reveal is a priestly ministry as a living reality, grounded securely through a threefold dynamic relationship. Its roots are in the mystery of the risen Lord and the Church. Its nature involves a mission of service to Christ and to the community. Its exercise occurs within the Church and its structures."

G.
Model for Homilies

This CBS News Commentary by Rod MacLeish is short (about one and a half minutes) and simply written. It is presented here as an example of clear writing to be emulated in short, daily homilies especially. (CBS Evening News, June 2, 1979. © 1979 CBS Inc. All rights reserved.)

ROD MacLEISH: Today, Caesar and God made a shaky compromise in Poland. Caesar has the guns, God has the Polish soul, and both sides have decided to settle for that.

This visit of Pope John II is, of course, an immense spiritual event. But it is also a political event, as symbolized by this afternoon's frosty meeting between the Pope and Edward Gierek, the man who runs Poland and its Communist Party, badly. As a Polish priest, bishop and cardinal, John Paul was a tough activist in the interminable jockeying feud between Church and Communist Party in this country, and he still is. Even non-beliving Poles tend to identify their intense nationalism with Christianity. Poland and the Polish Church began together nearly a thousand years ago. If it chose to, the Church could whip up massive active opposition to Poland's inept regime. In this square, this afternoon, the Pope delivered an impassioned sermon which stopped just short of inciting. And if it chose to, the Communist Party could obliterate the Church by brute force. But either extreme act would create flaming chaos in Poland and could invite Soviet intervention. Neither the Church nor the Party wants that.

The election of a Polish Pope last autumn made it inevitable that John Paul would visit this country. Given that inevitability, the

Caesars of the Polish Communist Party and God's Polish Pope decided to compromise on the small ground where they do agree. Poland's survival, which is something a little less than its happiness, is that small ground. So, not giving an inch and not being given an inch in the endless standoff between Church and Communist Party, Pope John Paul II came home to Poland today.

BIBLIOGRAPHY
Preaching

Books

Abbey, Merrill R., *Living Doctrine in a Vital Pulpit.* Abingdon, 1964.

Babin, E., *Week In and Week Out: A New Look at Liturgical Preaching.* Seabury, 1976.

Baillargeon, Anatole O., *Handbook for Special Preaching.* Herder and Herder, 1965.

_____, *New Media: New Forms, Contemporary Forms of Preaching.* Franciscan Herald, 1968.

Baird, John E., *Preparing for Platform and Pulpit.* Abingdon, 1974.

Baumann, J. Daniel, *An Introduction to Contemporary Preaching.* Baker, 1972.

Berton, Pierre, *The Comfortable Pew.* Lippincott, 1965.

Blackwood, Andrew W., *Planning a Year's Pulpit Work.* Abingdon, 1972.

_____, *Preparation of Sermons.* Abingdon, 1975.

Brack, Harold A., *Effective Oral Interpretation for Religious Leaders.* Prentice-Hall, 1964.

Brilioth, Yngve, *A Brief History of Preaching.* Fortress, 1965.

Brooks, Phillips, *Lectures on Preaching.* Baker, 1969.

Brown, Henry C., Jr., *et al., Steps to the Sermon.* Broadman, 1963.

Buber, Martin, *Between Man and Man.* Macmillan, 1965.

_____, *Gospel Power: Toward the Revitalization of Preaching.* Alba House, 1978.

Caemmerer, Richard, *Preaching for the Church.* Concordia, 1959.

Cooke, Bernard, *Ministry to Word and Sacraments.* Fortress, 1976.

Cox, James W., *A Guide to Biblical Preaching.* Abingdon, 1976.

Crum, Milton, *Manual on Preaching.* Judson, 1977.

Curran, Charles E., *The Crisis in Priestly Ministry.* Fides, 1972.

Davis, H. Grady, *Design for Preaching.* Fortress, 1958.

DeSales, Saint Francis, *On the Preacher and Preaching.* Regnery, 1964.

Echlin, Edward P., S.J., *The Priest as Preacher Past and Future.* Fides, 1973. 1973.

Edwards, Otis C., Jr., *The Living and Active Word.* Seabury, 1975.

Ehninger, D. (ed.), *Contemporary Rhetoric.* Scott-Foresman, 1972.

Erdahl, Lowell O., *Preaching for the People.* Abingdon, 1976.

Evans, William, *How To Prepare Sermons.* Moody, 1964.

Fant, Clyde E., *Preaching for Today.* Harper and Row, 1975.

Fant, Clyde E., and William M. Pinson, *Twenty Centuries of Great Preaching: An Encyclopedia of Preaching,* 13 vols. Word, 1971.

Fuller, Reginald, *What Is Liturgical Preaching?* SCM, 1957.

Funk, Robert W., *Language, Hermeneutic, and Word of God.* Harper and Row, 1966.

Grasso, Domenico, *Proclaiming God's Message: A Study in the Theology of Preaching.* Notre Dame, 1965.

Hall, E. T., *The Silent Language.* Fawcett, 1963.

Hall, Thor, *The Future Shape of Preaching.* Fortress, 1971.

Howe, Reuel L., *The Miracle of Dialogue.* Seabury, 1963.

———, *Partners in Preaching, Clergy and Laity in Dialogue.* Seabury, 1967.

Keir, Thomas H., *The Word in Worship: Preaching and Its Setting in Common Worship.* Oxford, 1962.

Killinger, John, *The Centrality of Preaching in the Total Task of the Ministry.* Word, 1969.

Lee, Charlotte I., *Oral Interpretation.* Houghton-Mifflin, 1965.

Lonergan, Bernard, *Method in Theology.* Herder and Herder, 1972.

MacNutt, Francis, *How To Prepare a Sermon.* Novalis, 1971.

McCurley, Foster R., *Proclaiming the Promise: Christian Preaching for the Old Testament.* Fortress, 1974.

McNamara, R. F., *Catholic Sunday Preaching: The American Guideliner for 1971–1975,* Word of God, 1975.

McNiel, Jesse J., *Preacher-Prophet in Mass Society.* Eerdmans, 1961.

Metz, Johann Baptist and Jean-Pierre Jossua (eds.), *The Crisis of Religious Language.* Herder and Herder, 1973 (*Concilium* 85).

Miller, Donald G., *Way to Biblical Preaching.* Abingdon, 1957.

Mills, Glen E., *Putting a Message Together.* Bobbs-Merrill, 1972.

Minear, P. S., "The Promise of His Coming," *Christian Hope and the Second Coming.* Seabury, 1978.

Mitchell, Henry H., *Recovery of Preaching.* Harper and Row, 1977.

Murphy, Roland, *Theology, Exegesis, and Proclamation.* Herder and Herder, 1971.

Nouwen, Henri J., *Creative Ministry.* Doubleday, 1971.

Ott, Heinrich, *Theology and Preaching.* Westminster, 1965.

Pennington, Basil, *God Has a Communication Problem: Creative Preaching Today.* Hawthorne, 1976.

Rahner, Hugo, *A Theology of Proclamation.* Herder, 1968.

Rahner, Karl (ed.), *Renewal of Preaching.* Paulist-Newman, 1968 (*Concilium* 33).

————, *The Word, Readings in Theology.* Kennedy, 1964.

Reese, James M., O.S.F.S., *Preaching God's Burning Word.* Liturgical, 1975.

Reid, Clyde, *The Empty Pulpit.* Harper and Row, 1967.

Rice, Charles L., *Interpretations and Imagination: The Preacher and Contemporary Literature.* Fortress, 1970.

Schmaus, Michael, *Preaching as a Saving Encounter.* Alba House, 1966.

Schramm, W., *Men, Messages, and Media.* Harper and Row, 1973.

Semmelroth, Otto, *The Preaching Word: On the Theology of Proclamation.* Herder and Herder, 1965.

Sittler, Joseph, *Anguish of Preaching.* Fortress, 1966.

Sleeth, Ronald E., *Persuasive Preaching.* Harper and Row, 1956.

Smith, Fred, *Communication and Culture.* Holt, Rinehart and Winston, 1975.

Standacher, Joseph M., *Laymen Proclaim the Word.* Franciscan, 1973.

Sweazey, George E., *Preaching the Good News.* Prentice-Hall, 1976.

Taylor, Gardner C., *How Shall They Preach?* Progressive Baptist, 1977.

Toohey, W. and W. D. Thompson (eds.), *Recent Homiletical Thought: A Bibliography, 1935–1965.* Abingdon, 1967.

Von Allmen, Jean-Jacques, *Preaching and Congregation.* John Knox, 1962.

Weaver, Carl H., *Human Listening: Processes and Behavior.* Bobbs-Merrill, 1972.

Weitz, S. (ed.), *Nonverbal Communication.* Oxford, 1974.

Welsh, Clement, *Preaching in a New Key.* Pilgrim, 1974.

Whitsell, F. and R. Perry, *Variety in Your Preaching.* Revell, 1954.

Young, Henry James (ed.), *Preaching on Suffering and Love.* Fortress, 1978.

Articles

Barrosse, Thomas, C.S.C., "The Preacher's Role as Exegete," *Preaching Today (A Journal of Homiletics),* Spring 1965.

Bell, Michael, "Preaching in Our Mass Environment," *Preaching* IV (Jan.-Feb. 1969), pp. 1–27.

Bishop, John, "How To Construct a Sermon," *Preaching Today (A Journal of Homiletics),* Vol. 1, No. 3, May-June 1966.

Brown, R. E., "Hermeneutics," *Jerome Biblical Commentary,* eds. Raymond E. Brown, S.S., Joseph A. Fitzmeyer, S.J., Roland E. Murphy, O. Carm., Vol. II (The New Testament and Topical Articles), pp. 71, 80–102 (especially 93–99).

Burghardt, Walter, "The Word Made Flesh Today," *New Catholic World,* Vol. 221, No. 1323, May/June 1978. Entire issue on Preaching. See also for sermon models Burghardt's book *Tell The Next Generation* (Paulist Press, 1980).

Byrnes, Joseph, "Preaching: Present Possibilities and Perennial Value," *Worship* XLII, January 1968, pp. 14–21.

Curran, Charles A. "The Psychology of Audience Reaction: Personal Change Through Sermons," *Proceedings of the Catholic Homiletic Society,* 1960.

Dance, F. X., "Communication Theory, Hope for a Sagging Pulpit?" *Preaching Today,* Vol. 6, No. 2, March-April 1971, pp. 12–15.

_____, "Communication Theory and Contemporary Preaching," *Preaching Today (A Journal of Homiletics),* Vol. 3, No. 4, 1968.

Dayton, Donald W., and Lucile Sider, "Women as Preachers: Evangelical Precedents," *Christianity Today,* Vol. XIX, No. 17, 1975.

Doss, Richard and M. Michael Pugh, "Preaching and the Principles of Stanislavski," *Preaching Today (A Journal of Homiletics),* Vol. 4, No. 3, 1969.

Duffy, Regis, "The Deafening Question," *Liturgy,* Vol. 19, No. 5, May 1974.

Fillichin, Ralph, "I Sleep While You Preach," *Preaching Today (A Journal of Homiletics),* Vol. 5, No. 2, 1970.

Fitzmyer, J. A., "Belief in Jesus Today," *Commonweal,* November 1974, pp. 137–142.

Fosdick, Harry Emerson, ed., "How I Prepare My Sermon," *Quarterly Journal of Speech* XI, February 1954, pp. 49–62.

_____, "What Is the Matter With Preaching?" *Preaching Today (A Journal of Homiletics),* Vol. 2, No. 1, March 1967.

Fuller, R. H., "Preparing the Homily," *Worship* 48 (Oct. 1974), pp. 442–457.

Graham, William, "A Personal Approach to Preaching," *Preaching Today (A Journal of Homiletics),* Vol. 3, No. 3, 1968.

Haller, Eduard, "On the Interpretative Task," *Interpretation* XXI (1967), pp. 158–166.

Hart, Nelson, "A Simple Style: One Basis for Effective Preaching," *Preaching Today (A Journal of Homiletics),* Vol. 1, No. 6, Nov.-Dec. 1966.

Horne, Chevis, "Let the Sermon Be Empowered," *Preaching Today (A Journal of Homiletics),* Vol. 5, No. 5, 1970.

_____, "The Preacher Who Knows Pain," *Preaching Today (A Journal of Homiletics),* Vol. 4, No. 2, 1969.

Howe, Revel, "The Responsibility of the Preaching Task," *Preaching Today (A Journal of Homiletics),* Vol. 4, No. 5, 1969.

Jabusch, Willard, "De-Mythologizing the Image of the Preacher," *Preaching Today (A Journal of Homiletics),* Vol. 3, No. 3, 1968.

————, "The Preacher as Artist," *Preaching Today (A Journal of Homiletics),* Vol. 5, No. 3, 1970.

Kahlefeld, H., "The Pericope and Preaching," *Concilium* 10 (1965), pp. 39–51.

Keck, Leander, "Listening To and Listening For," *Interpretation* (1973), pp. 184–202.

Lee, Dr. Charlotte, "The Who, Why, and What of Sharing the Word of God," *Preaching Today (A Journal of Homiletics),* Vol. 5, No. 1, 1970.

Logal, Nelson W., "Turning Off the Word," *Homiletic and Pastoral Review,* October 1977.

McCarty, S., "Homiletic or Hermeneutic," *Bible Today,* March 1973.

Malcomson, William, "The Preaching Event," *Preaching Today (A Journal of Homiletics),* Vol. 4, No. 5, 1969.

Meador, Prentice, "Toward an Understanding of Today's Listener," *Preaching Today (A Journal of Homiletics),* Vol. 2, No. 5, 1967.

Mezger, K., "Preparation for Preaching," *Journal for Theology and Church* 2 (1965), pp. 159–179.

Milner, A. P. (ed.), "The Ministry of the Word," *New Blackfriars* 49 (1967-68).

Murphy, David M., "Inductive Preaching: Reaching People Where They Are," *The Priest,* June 1978, pp. 11–14.

Padavano, Anthony, "What Are They Saying About God?" *Preaching Today (A Journal of Homiletics),* Vol. 2, No. 6, 1967.

Rahner, K. (ed.), "The Renewal of Preaching," *Concilium* 33 (1968).

Stendahl, Krister, "Implications of Form-Criticism and Tradition-Criticism for Biblical Interpretation," *Journal of Biblical Literature* 77 (1958), pp. 33–38.

Tang, Emery, "Understanding the Listener," *Provincial Annals* XXIX (April 1969), pp. 15–19.

Thompson, W. D., "Testing the Audience Analysis Skills of Ministers," *Preaching* IV (May-June 1969), pp. 1–7.

Toombs, Lawrence E., "The Problematic of Preaching from the Old Testament," *Interpretation* XXIII (1969), pp. 302–314.

Weiss, Daniel E., "St. Augustine and the Preacher's Personal Proof," *Preaching Today (A Journal of Homiletics),* Vol. 2, No. 2, 1967.

Communication:
Theory and Practice

Books

Abbey, Merrill R., *Communication in Pulpit and Parish.* Westminster, 1973.

Adler, Mortimer, *The Difference of Man and the Difference It Makes.* Holt, Rinehart and Winston, 1967.

Andersen, Martin, *et al., The Speaker and His Audience.* Harper and Row, 1964.

Brooks, Keith, *The Communicative Arts and Sciences of Speech.* Merrill, 1967.

Brown, Roger, *Words and Things.* Free, 1958.

Bryant, Donald C., and Karl R. Wallace, *Oral Communication: A Short Course in Speaking.* Appleton-Century-Crofts, 1954.

Cherry, Colin, *On Human Communication.* John Wiley, 1961.

Clevenger, Theodore, Jr., *Audience Analysis.* Bobbs-Merrill, 1966.

Dance, Frank (ed.), *Human Communication Theory: Original Essays.* Holt, Rinehart and Winston, 1967.

Dance, Frank, and Carl E. Larson, *Speech Communication: Concepts and Behavior.* Holt, Rinehart and Winston, 1972.

_____, *The Functions of Human Communication: A Theoretical Approach.* Holt, Rinehart and Winston, 1976.

De Sola, Pool, *et al.* (eds.) *Handbook of Communication.* Rand-McNally, 1973.

Dexter, Lewis and David White, *People, Society and Mass Communication.* Free, 1964.

Gray, Giles and Claude Wise, *The Bases of Speech.* Harper, 1959.

Hall, Edward T., *The Silent Language.* Fawcett, 1961.

Hovland, Carl *et al., Communication and Persuasion.* Yale, 1959.

Jackson, B. J. (ed.), *Communication: Learning for Churchmen.* Abingdon, 1968.

————, *Television, Radio, Film for Churchmen.* Abingdon, 1969.

————, *Audiovisual Facilities and Equipment for Churchmen.* Abingdon, 1970.

Klapper, Joseph T., *The Effects of Mass Communication.* Free, 1961.

Knapp, Mark L., *Nonverbal Communication in Interpersonal Relations.* Holt, Rinehart and Winston, 1970.

Lee, Irving J., *How To Talk with People.* Harper, 1952.

McLuhan, Marshall, *Understanding Media.* McGraw-Hill, 1964.

Miller, Glen E., *Putting the Message Together.* Bobbs-Merrill, 1972.

————, *Explorations in Interpersonal Communication.* Sage, 1976.

Powers, David Guy, *Fundamentals in Speech.* McGraw-Hill, 1951.

Smith, Alfred G., *Communication and Culture.* Holt, Rinehart and Winston, 1966.

Vygotsky, L. S., *Thought and Language.* Wiley, 1962.

Zelko, Harold P. and Frank Dance, *Business and Professional Speech Communication.* Holt, Rinehart and Winston, 1965 (Chapter 6).

Article

"Speech Communication: The Sign of Mankind," in *Symposium on Human Language in the Yearbook of the Great Books of the Western World, The Great Ideas Today.* Encyclopaedia Britannica, 1975.

Books on Writing and Expression

Dillon, David, *Writing Experience and Expression.* Heath, 1976.

Lambuth, David *et al., The Golden Book on Writing.* Penguin, 1976.

Strunk, W., Jr., and White, E. B., *The Elements of Style.* Macmillan, 1972.

Books on Black Preaching

Cleland, James, *Preaching To Be Understood.* Abingdon, 1965.

Golden, James L. and R. E. Rieke, *The Rhetoric of Black Americans.* Merrill, 1971.

Hamilton, Charles F., *The Black Preacher in America.* Morrison, 1972.

Mays, Benjamin, *The Negro's God, As Reflected in His Literature,* Negro, 1969.

Mitchell, Henry H., *Black Preaching.* Lippincott, 1970.

Encyclopedia Articles

"History of Preaching," *The New Catholic Encyclopedia*. McGraw-Hill, 1967, Vol. 11, pp. 684ff.

"Homiletics," *The New Catholic Encyclopedia*. McGraw-Hill, 1967, Vol. 7, pp. 111f.

"Homily," *The New Catholic Encyclopedia*. McGraw-Hill, 1967, Vol. 7, pp. 113f.

"Preaching," *Sacramentum Mundi*. Herder and Herder, 1970, Vol. 5, pp. 81ff.

"Preaching (Homiletic Theory)," *The New Catholic Encyclopedia*. McGraw-Hill, 1967, Vol. 11, pp. 690ff.

"Theology of Preaching," *The New Catholic Encyclopedia,* McGraw-Hill, 1967, Vol. 11, pp. 697ff.

Church Documents

Constitution on the Sacred Liturgy *(Sacrosanctum Concilium)*, Chap. 1 (Sections I and II), Chap. 2.

Decree on the Bishops' Pastoral Office in the Church *(Christus Dominus)*, Chap. 2.

Decree on the Ministry and Life of Priests *(Presbyterorum Ordinis)*, Chap. 1, Chap. 2 (Section I), Chap. 3 (Section I).

Dogmatic Constitution on Divine Revelation *(Dei Verbum)*, Chap. 2, Chap. 6.

Dogmatic Constitution on the Church *(Lumen Gentium)*, Chap. 3.

Homily Services and Resources*

Good News, Joseph T. Nolan (ed.), 1229 So. Santos St., Los Angeles, Cal. 90015 (homilies, ideas, scriptural and contemporary illustrations, introduction to the word).

Guide for the Christian Assembly, Thierry Maertens and Jean Frisque, Notre Dame, Fides (exegesis of Sundays and holy days; theological reflections on readings).

Homilies, Diocese of Lansing, Mich. Liturgical Co., 300 West Ottawa St.,

---

* Some of these services include liturgical aids, sacramental celebrations, services for children and special religious and civic occasions, stories, images, ideas and reflections.

Lansing, Mich. 48933 (exegesis of Sundays and weekdays, with short reflections on the readings).

Homily Helps, Leonard Foley, O.F.M. (ed.), St. Anthony Messenger Press, 1615 Republic St., Cincinnati, Ohio 45219 (exegesis for Sundays and holy days with homily reflections).

Homily Hints, Capsulized Communications, Box 70, Dorion, Quebec, Can. J7V 2J5 (thematic introductions, contemporary expressions of the theme).

Homily Service, Virginia Sloyan (ed.), Liturgical Conference, 1313 Massachusetts Ave. N.W., Wash. D.C. 20005 (exegesis, homilies for Sundays and holy days).

Markings, Michael F. McCauley, Thomas More Association, 180 No. Wabash, Chicago, Ill. 60601 (exegetical resources, homiletic reflections for Sundays and holy days).

Nova et Vetera, Joseph P. LoCigno (ed.), 37 Evergreen Place, E. Orange, N.J. 07018 (Sundays and holy days, exegesis and homilies).

Preaching the New Lectionary: The Word of God for the Church Today, Reginald H. Fuller, Liturgical Press, 1974 (collection of three cycles of lectionary readings, with exegesis and reflections for homilies).

Proclamation: Aids for Interpreting the Lessons of the Church Year (Protestant), Fortress Press, Philadelphia, Pa. (three year cycle of lessons used by Protestant Episcopal Church, Roman Catholic Church, The United Church of Christ, the Lutheran and Presbyterian Churches and other denominations (exegesis, homily ideas).

Service, Paulist Press, 545 Island Road, Ramsey, N.J. 07446 (exegesis of Sundays and holy days, Scripture reflections, homilies, doctrinal themes and practical application).

Word and Witness (Protestant), Sunday Publications, Inc., 3003 S. Congress Avenue, Palm Springs, Fla. 33461 (exegesis of Sunday readings, ideas and images and sermons).